TERRIBLE NERD

KEVIN SAVETZ

ISBN: 978-1-939169-00-6 (printed edition)
      978-1-939169-01-3 (ebook edition)

Cover art by David Simmer II of Blogography.com.
Edited by Devanie Angel.
George Beker's bot cartoons on page 98 are copyrighted by Beker and used with permission.

First edition

Published by
Savetz Publishing
www.SavetzPublishing.com
www.TerribleNerd.com

Dedicated to the women in my life.
In order of appearance:
Mom, Colleen, Devanie, Peace, Zoë, and Camelia.

CHAPTER 0

My generation was the first one to have access to computers at such a young age. In the early 1980s, middle class kids could get their hands on Apple //s and Commodore 64s, Atari 800s and TRS-80s, and other machines that offered the kind of computing power that would have been impossible just a few years before. While that level of power did exist just a few years before, it wouldn't have been able to fit on your desk, nor was it affordable to anyone other than a university, corporation, or government. Here we were, kids embarking on the threshold of a whole new thing, which for us started out as a hobby, or a toy to play games on, and for many of us, ended up being our careers, sometimes defining the course of our lives.

My generation was the first to never handle a slide rule (except as a curiosity), because we were the first to have electronic calculators. We were the last to enjoy the smell of mimeographed worksheets in school, because of photocopiers. We were the first kids to enjoy home video games, MTV, and microwave ovens.

Who am I? I'm just a 41-year-old nerd, one of a bazillion kids who grew up amidst the amazing explosion of microchip-based technology that started in the 1970s — pocket electronic calculators, home computers, Speak & Spells. You might know me from my Web sites for retrocomputing hobbyists, AtariMagazines.com and AtariArchives .org. Or maybe you know me from my business, Savetz Publishing, where I create useful Web sites for consumers and small businesses: like printable documents and templates at FreePrintable.net, and the free fax-sending service FaxZero.com.

Or maybe you don't know me at all. I'm just another nerd. Here are the basics: I was born in 1971 in Southern California. My parents divorced when I was two. Mom remarried when I was four and we moved to a brand-new house in the San Fernando Valley city of Agoura, California. The kitchen appliances were green and I had my own room.

PART 1

CHAPTER 1
AEROSPACE

When I was a little kid, I was into airplanes. Lots of little boys are, right? When Mom, stepdad Joe, and I moved into that new house, I got to pick my room's wallpaper (airplanes) and paint color (sky blue). My room was decorated with pictures of airplanes, model planes, and airplane mobiles hanging from the ceiling.

Joe was employed at Litton Industries, an aerospace company. My grandfather was retired from his work at Rocket Jet, another aerospace company. So, my room was decorated with planes. I had a picture of the Space Shuttle riding piggyback on a 747, and a photo of Neil Armstrong on the moon. There was a cool photograph of that Cold War plane with the ginormous round antenna on top. I had models of spy planes — not crappy put-it-together-yourself plastic models but the same heavy, metal models that aerospace guys had on their desks at the office.

The bounty of Joe's work didn't end there. My bedside drawer held a pile of decommissioned books, still marked "top secret," with drawings of rockets and missiles and planes and guns. I had a button that was supposedly from the avionics deck of the Space Shuttle Enterprise. Still have that, actually.

Joe did a lot of secret stuff at his work, so couldn't talk about most of what he did. But the stuff I did see was intriguing. A big part of his job was making models and mock-ups (a mock-up is a full-size model, as opposed to a scaled-down version) of emerging government tech. I saw pictures of the "Star Wars" space-based Earth protection system, probably before it was given the politically friendly name Strategic Defense Initiative. One evening, Joe brought home a pair of night-vision goggles (the goggles were called "Starbright," and could have easily cost $10,000, if you could buy a set at all, which you couldn't). My friend Michael and I played with the goggles in the garage and street in front of the house. Just two kids running in the street with secret military tech.

Joe would sometimes take me to plastics shops, the places where he bought the raw materials for creating models and mock-ups of things that destroy things. The places were impressive, with towering spires of plastic rods in every color and diameter. One day, Joe brought home a Polaroid picture of a bloody, severed hand on a table saw. It was disgusting and totally cool, something he made at work as a joke. Then he pulled the fake severed hand from his briefcase. I brought the Polaroid to school the next day

4

and showed it to all of my friends, somehow managing to not get caught with it by the teachers.

Joe worked near Van Nuys Airport, and Mom would take me to the airport to watch the planes take off and land. In the time that we lived together, I got to go to his workplace exactly once, during a family open house day. I saw his office for about 10 seconds. I was told not to go in because it hadn't been cleared of secret stuff, but I walked in anyway. And I saw … nothing. A desk with some parts on it.

My mom and me at the Litton Industries open house. I'm playing with some sort of light pen.

Joe was also involved in a project called the Pip Projector, which was a semi-portable video player that was intended to be used for training. It would show a video that gave the viewer several options (such as press "A" if you should call for backup, press "B" if you should fire your weapon, "C" if you should negotiate with the suspect) and then showed different videos based on your choice. I don't know how the technology worked, but this was a few years before laser discs made that sort of thing more widespread. Joe and I did not get along well. We had good moments, but a lot of the time that we lived in the same house — from when I was four until the day after I graduated high school — was tense. He could generally be counted on to buy me stuff, but he could not be counted on to understand me, or to be kind. I knew from when I was little that he was not a kind man. Unfortunately it took Mom a lot longer to figure that out.

My dad — Steve — and I were buddies, but I only got to see him every other weekend. At that time, Dad taught electronics and drafting at Palisades High School. He took me to his school one day when I was four or five. The girls in the drafting class fawned over me, and then I got to play with the ham radio in the electronics lab. Dad was such a geek, he had a ham radio in his classroom. In a few years, Dad's geekiness would turn to computers.

CHAPTER 2
ELEMENTARY SCHOOL

For as nerdy as I am, sometimes I am a terrible nerd, and someone should revoke my membership. Case in point: I haven't read Lord of the Rings, and I haven't seen the movies. Another early example: Star Wars.

I was in first grade when Star Wars hit the theaters. My mom took me to see it, but I didn't like it that much. I didn't understand a lot of what was going on. But the other boys in Mrs. Brass' first grade class went Star Wars crazy. Every game was Skywalker this and Darth that, and I just felt ambivalent about the whole thing. It occurs to me now that the other kids might not have understood a whole lot of what was going on in that movie either, but so what? Lightsabers! 'Splody battles in space! Yoda! (Well, shoot, Wikipedia says that Yoda didn't appear until The Empire Strikes Back — see, I am a terrible nerd.)

Also in first grade: dinosaurs. Little kids' fixation with dinosaurs wasn't just a '70s thing, of course. Kids in grade school today still love their dinos. In first grade, you had to have a favorite dinosaur. You needed to pick your allegiance. I didn't care about dead reptiles too much, but DECLINE TO STATE/NO PREFERENCE were not legitimate checkboxes, if indeed there were checkboxes, in the world of first graders. It seemed like the default dino to back was the T. rex, but he was all bite-y and always getting into fights, and just seemed like the bully of the Cretaceous period. So when pressed for a favorite, I chose the Brontosaurus. The Brontosaurus had sleek lines, and seemed to like nothing more than to quietly munch on plants while the Tyrannosaurus Rexes duked it out over by the Sleestak huts.

So I imagined that I'd checked the imaginary checkbox that said BRONTOSAURUS.

Years later, the imaginary Department of Paleo Affairs sent back my form with a big red stamp reading INVALID CHOICE. The Brontosaurus isn't even a dinosaur anymore; apparently the powers that be renamed it "Apatosaurus." I can't even pick a real, live extinct animal. I'm a terrible nerd.

And don't get me started about Pluto.

✳ ✳ ✳

In first and second grade, I was in a special P.E. class. I was pulled out into Mr. Moon's physical education class because I couldn't catch a ball, or throw one, or do much of anything physical, I guess. It was often just me and a deaf, learning-disabled kid from the other school that shared the same parking lot. Mr. Moon was nice, and patient with me, unlike every other P.E. teacher I had after that. The little class of physically uneducated kids spent a lot of time pushing ourselves around on rolling skateboard things, and practicing catching and throwing balls.

Many years later, I learned that Mr. Moon went from school to school doing the Special P.E. thing all around the area. Miles away at his private school for rich kids, Danny, a boy who would become one of my best friends, was also enduring sessions with Mr. Moon.

Eventually I graduated Mr. Moon's P.E. class and became a general disappointment and perennial last-pick in the regular P.E. class. I pretty much forgot about him until the last week of fifth grade, when he reappeared, big red bouncy ball in hand. It was a final follow-up before I left for middle school. He said that if I could catch and throw the ball with him 10 times without missing, he would buy me a six-pack of whatever soda I wanted.

I thought that with such high stakes on the line, Mr. Moon had no faith that I could actually accomplish that task. I failed. Luckily, like geometry and cursive writing, throwing and catching a big red ball was not a skill that I would actually need later in life.

Words, on the other hand, were things that I would need later in life. What I lacked in physical education skills, I made up for in reading skills. In first grade, I pegged the meter in the standardized reading level tests. The results said that I was reading at grade level 9.9, which was as high as the system would score. The teachers tried to slow me down, to keep me from reading at reading time. Maybe I could help the other kids read, they suggested. My mom went ballistic. "I don't care if he's reading the dictionary — give my kid a book and let him read it." Oddly enough, in second or third grade when we started learning phonics, that made me cry. I could sight-read at a 10th grade level, but I couldn't get my head around the whole phonics thing. I'm not sure why they made me endure the phonics lessons, but it was a terrible part of my day.

I've always loved reading and enjoyed writing, probably because they came naturally to me. In fourth or fifth grade, I decided to put my writing talents to a truly important task, writing an epic tome that would benefit my classmates and other children for generations to come: The Bad Word Dictionary. The Bad Word Dictionary was an alphabetized list of curse words, each complete with definitions and sample sentences.

I was maybe ten handwritten pages into that project before I was found out. The teacher took the pages away from me. I was mortified, sure that she would call my parents after school and then hell would rain down on me. The call didn't come that night, or the next. Was she too busy to ruin my life? Maybe she threw the pages away without ever seeing the terrible words and ideas that they contained? I don't know, but my theory today is that the pages were so clueless and awful that they ended up in the teachers' lounge for the staff to snicker at. My nascent career as the Noah Webster of grade school cursing came to an abrupt end, which was probably for the best.

FAIRCHILD CHANNEL F

When I was little — five or six years old — Mom and Joe bought a Fairchild Channel F video game system. The Channel F was released in August 1976 for $169.95, and was the first video game system to use programmable cartridges. Even before the Atari 2600, you could insert cartridges, which looked like orange 8-track tapes, into this machine and play different games. I liked the bright cartridges. Dad had an 8-track tape player (on which he played Gordon Lightfoot and bluegrass,) so I thought they were cool.

The Channel F was hooked up to the big TV in our living room. We had several games for it, including a tic-tac-toe game that, when it won, displayed YOU LOSE TURKEY on the screen. For a while, I thought that calling someone a turkey was about the meanest thing you could say. One day some kid was harassing me on the playground at Lupin Hill Elementary School, so I called him a turkey, inspired by the salty language I had picked up from Channel F Videocart 1 (Tic-Tac-Toe, Shooting Gallery, Doodle, Quadra-Doodle). The bully was incredulous. "Did you just call me turkey?!" He didn't know what to make of me, and left me alone.

Playing the Channel F was often a family activity. I'd play Baseball (Videocart 12) with Joe, and Hangman (Videocart 18) with Mom. Looking at Wikipedia's list of games for that system, I notice that only 26 cartridges were released. I can't imagine Nintendo or Xbox limiting themselves to 26 games a year, let alone over the lifetime of a product.

My favorite games were probably Quadra-Doodle and Maze. Quadra-Doodle let you draw on the screen, but it would mirror the art like a kaleidoscope. There was a mode where the game itself would do the drawing, letting you zone out while it created weird, low-resolution kaleidoscopic art. Maze (Videocart 10) drew a maze on the screen, and you'd move your little square around trying to find your way out. You can try these games on your PC — the Multi Emulator Super System emulator can play Channel F games and those from other systems.

One thing that an emulator cannot emulate is the Channel F's strange controllers. The top of the joystick could be pushed in eight directions, but you could also twist it left and right. You could push down on the top, or pull up on it. There were a lot of axes of movement packed into that controller — it worked as a joystick and a paddle — but it was kind of a terrible controller. It's easy to say that in hindsight: after all, truly inspired game controls like the classic Atari joystick and the Nintendo D-pad came after. But even at the time, little kids like me knew that this joystick was lacking in ergonomics, though we didn't know the word yet.

But the games were fun. The shooting gallery game (Videocart 1 again) provided hours of entertainment. Addition & Subtraction Math Quiz (Videocart 6), not so much.

One day, I invited a girl from my class home after school. We might have been in third grade at the time. We played Channel F games together. A parental unit made us bowls of strawberries with sugar on top for a snack. I remember hearing someone say, "It's puppy love." Which it wasn't at all — I just wanted someone to play video games with.

Sadly (and perhaps unsurprisingly) this is the only time until college that a girl will appear in the pages of this book. There simply wasn't a lot of intersection between my young nerdy life and my nascent love life. That afternoon in elementary school, I pretty much exhausted the chances that computers and video games would give me to connect with girls.

The Channel F had a permanent place connected to the living room TV until April 1980 when I came down with chicken pox. The game unit was moved up to my room, a relocation which ended up being permanent. I'm not sure why I was allowed to have a TV in my room, but we shouldn't look gift horses in the mouth.

In 1979, the Fairchild company abandoned the Channel F system and sold the technology to a company called Zircon. Zircon kept the system viable for a while longer, releasing a new version of the hardware and some more games. I was concerned that our video game system was obsolete, and wrote a letter to consumer advocate David Horowitz, asking him to look into it. David hosted a TV show called Consumer Buyline. He replied with a pre-printed postcard thanking me for the suggestion. I was thrilled with that, the way only a little kid can be thrilled with receiving a pre-printed postcard. David "Fight Back! And don't let anyone rip you off!" Horowitz couldn't prepare me for one of the fundamental truths of technology: that tech gets obsolete. The Channel F system hardware was created primarily by a man named Jerry Lawson. Some 30 years after his video game allowed me to get a girl in front of the 27" Zenith in our wood-paneled living room, I met Jerry. We were at a Vintage Computer Festival conference in Mountain View, California. I was going to give a presentation that day, so was loitering around the public area talking to other conference-goers. Two men were sitting, chatting, and I joined them. One introduced himself: it was Jerry. He was old but sharp. We talked about the Channel F; and about POW!, a weird little TV show based around the Channel F. I was thrilled to meet and talk with the man who invented — not *the* first home video game system, but *my* first home video game system. He had even been a member of the Homebrew Computer Club, which was an early computer hobbyist group in Silicon Valley, famous in tech circles. Jerry was the man.

The other man we were talking to introduced himself as John. He seemed like a character: smart but with an unusual take on things, and an unruly white beard. After talking with them for a half an hour or so, Jerry Lawson on one side and this John fellow on the other, I figured out that John was John Draper. I was chatting with two legends, sandwiched between Mr. Channel F and Captain Crunch, a pioneer of phone phreaking and computer hacking.

A year later, at the next Vintage Computer Festival, I saw Jerry for the last time. He was recovering from a stroke and didn't look so steady that time around. I was saddened when Jerry died in 2011.

In 1981, I got an Intellivision for Christmas, a new video game that I desperately wanted and for which I was grateful. But the downside was that the Channel F unceremoniously disappeared from the house: Mom gave it away. But it's OK; I have my own now, along with 24 of the 26 cartridges, including a couple that are signed by Jerry. I'm still missing Videocart 19: Checkers and Videocart 20: Video Whizball. I've waited a very long time to find out what a Whizball is, exactly.

INTELLIVISION

The Atari 2600 was a cornerstone of video game history, and one that I almost completely passed by. A few of my friends had one, and the games were fun enough when I played them at their houses. At home, though, I was happy with the Channel F. The graphics were crude, but seemed comparable to the early Atari 2600 games. Later games, especially those from Activision and Imagic, did make the 2600 hardware shine. But in 1980, Pitfall and Kaboom! didn't exist yet. My friends played blocky games like Combat, Air-Sea Battle, and Canyon Bomber on their Ataris.

So while I'd never, never opt to go play outside when a friend's Atari was an option, at home I was happy with my Channel F. Until I saw the Intellivision, that is.

The graphics on the new Intellivision game systems were incredible. Nothing like the chunky graphics on the 2600 and Fairchild, images on the Intellivision were colorful and detailed. There was a baseball game in which the outfielders ran out to the field at the beginning of the game, their arms and legs moving realistically, to the roar of a cheering crowd. There was a card game in which the dealer's eyes moved back and forth back shiftily as he flung the cards onto the green felt. I lobbied hard for an Intellivision for Christmas.

When an Intellivision appeared under the Christmas tree in 1981, there wasn't a happier kid around. My parents got me Armor Battle, Space Battle, Sea Battle. . . and maybe even some non-battle related games. I connected it to the TV in my room where the Fairchild used to be.

My favorite games over the years included Shark! Shark!, with gameplay that remains unique — or at least, hasn't been copied a million times. In the game, you control a little fish. As you swim around the ocean eating smaller fish, your fish grows (thus enabling it to eat bigger fish). You could only kill the titular shark by biting its tail a number of times. It was a fun little game that could be played alone or with a friend.

Another favorite was Tron: Solar Sailer. That was one of just four talking games for the console. (The talking games required an add-on gadget called Intellivoice, which I must have gotten in 1982 as a birthday gift.) Wikipedia says that Tron: Solar Sailer only sold 70,000 copies (the worst of the speech games), and then goes on to explain what made it complicated and boring. Well, I liked it and the high-tech, inside-of-a-computer graphics. Of the hours and hours that I played that game, I saw a strange bug exactly once, in which the vehicle I was controlling went flying off of the grid on which it was supposed to be locked. It sort of flew in nothingness for a while, then found its way back to another grid. I tried and tried to reproduce the bug but was never able to. Decades later, at a Classic Gaming Expo in Las Vegas, I asked the game's programmer, Keith Robinson, about the bug. He confirmed that it was indeed a rare bug. He told me that a playtester had discovered the problem during development, and showed him a replay of the bug in action, because they videotaped all of the playtesting sessions. He went back to the computer and fixed the bug, or so he thought. But the version of the game that was released does rarely display the fly-off-the-grid bug. Keith told me that he has never seen the bug "in the wild" on the released version of the game. I felt vindicated, and happy to have spotted something in a favorite game that most players never would see.

I pored over the Intellivision game catalogs obsessively. Once, Mom caught me reading the catalog in church. That did not go over well. She took the catalog away, which totally sucked because it was the new catalog with the black cover, which featured games that weren't in the older, blue-cover catalog.

Despite God's disapproval, my game collection grew and grew over the years. Every birthday, every Christmas was an opportunity for another game or two. In 1982, for my 11th birthday, Mom got me a birthday cake with a Space Armada screenshot done in the icing. (Space Armada was Intellivision's ripoff of Space Invaders.) I loved the cake, and it was a hit among friends at my birthday party. When Mom tried to have the cake company do another video game screenshot cake the next year, they refused — they were concerned about violating the copyright.

Space Armada on a cake for my 11th birthday.

When my friend Michael got a Nintendo Entertainment System, he ditched his Intellivision and gave me his games. That score meant I had duplicates of some games, but also added Q*Bert and Astrosmash to my collection. Q*Bert was a great adaption of the arcade game — but if you played it for too long, an optical illusion would make the playfield seem to be upside-down, which meant imminent death. Astrosmash, widely regarded as one of the best Intellivision games, was a fast-paced space shoot-em-up that you could play for hours.

Not all of the games that I got over the years were as good. I wanted to like Truckin', in which you played the part of a truck driver making deliveries, but it turns out that a game that involves long stretches of driving in a straight line is pretty boring.

I did like Loco Motion, a puzzle game, but it was infested with bugs that made it difficult to play. I wanted to like Donkey Kong, but it was terrible compared to the arcade version and the ColecoVision version. Released in 1982, ColecoVision was Intellivision's rival. When you bought a ColecoVision, Donkey Kong was the game that came with it. The Coleco version of Donkey Kong was fantastic. One popular theory is that Coleco deliberately made the Intellivision version inferior so people would buy a ColecoVision. I recently learned that in 2011 a homebrewer created a fantastic Intellivision version of Donkey Kong. (www.intellivision.us/intvgames/dkarcade/dkarcade.php)

I also enjoyed B-17 Bomber, another one of the talking Intellivision games. I discovered a bug where if you got a very low negative score (by relentlessly bombing your own territory), strange characters would appear in place of the score digits. It's amazing that, in those days before downloadable software updates, bugs were so rare. It was rewarding to find bugs — discovering something and most other players would never see, and having thought of a possibility that the programmer didn't expect. Sometimes, when my friends and I wanted to try to create problems with games, we'd insert the cartridge only halfway, or tap the reset button a dozen times to try to confuse the hardware into behaving unpredictably. These experiments would cause strange graphics and sounds on the TV.

One day, a parental unit took me to the mall to see what new Intellivision games were out. There, the man behind the counter demonstrated the Intellivision Keyboard Component, an add-on that would turn the Intellivision into a computer. He showed us how you could play games from cartridges or from cassette tapes. I don't remember which cassette programs he showed us, but looking at the list online — they include thrilling titles such as Conversational French, Jack LaLanne's Physical Conditioning, Spelling Challenge, and Jeane Dixon Astrology — you can imagine how compelling it must have been. The Keyboard Component was never released ... at least, not widely so. I don't know if the keyboard was for sale that day or was only being demonstrated. But I saw it that day, and it would be worth a small fortune to a collector today.

Flash forward to 1989: I did something stupid before leaving for college. I put an ad in the Recycler newspaper and sold my Intellivision and what was by then a massive collection of games. I figured I would need the money for school. (I got the game console in 1981, and was still playing it when getting ready to move away to college eight years later. That machine had some staying power.) I missed the games, and bought another Intellivision not too many years later.

Today, as a collector, my continued lack of lust for the 2600 serves me well. It's a heck of a lot easier — and cheaper — to collect the entire Intellivision game catalog (around 125 games) than the 2600 library, which tops 400 games, or arguably many more, depending on how you count them. My Intellivision cartridge collection includes all but 20 cartridges: the ones I'm lacking are primarily super-rare titles like Scooby Doo's Maze Chase and Tutankham. (I had originally written "titles like Scooby Doo's Maze Chase and The Jetsons' Ways with Words," but I looked on eBay and found the Jetsons game for sale at a reasonable price. I bought the game and had to re-write this.)

MOM'S NOTEBOOK

My mom wrote letters to me, in a thin composition note-book, sporadically from 1978 (when I was seven) through 1984 (when I was 13). Most of it is sweet stuff about what I was doing at camp, updates on my retainer and braces, our visits to Grandma in Arizona, and family health issues. Just a couple of entries mention my interest in computers.

In August 1980, a few weeks before I would start fourth grade, she wrote: "Kevin, today you decided to buy yourself a $400 computer. On 75 cents a week [allowance] this could be quite a project. You don't know this but Dad [Joe] and I are against it. You are too young at the moment. I wonder if you'll still love computers when you get older." (That same day, she also wrote: "Today you started asking a lot of questions on reproduction. You've asked before but this time I couldn't put you off. So now you know.")

The entry on October 27, 1980 simply says: "Kevin you are sometimes a real pain in the rear."

November 24, 1982, 6th grade: "You are still playing guitar and doing very well. Maybe one day you will be a famous entertainer. I doubt it very much unless a computer guitar comes into the future. All you talk about is computer games and video equipment. Sometimes it really gets boring."

CHAPTER 3
ATARI 800

One day in 1982, during the drive from my house in Agoura to my dad's for our weekend together, he mentioned that he was thinking of getting a computer. Dad had used some computers at the school where he worked, which was his first exposure to personal computing. He wanted one of his own. He did some research and decided on the Atari 800, and I wholeheartedly agreed. He briefly considered the Commodore 64, but the Atari had better graphics and sound — it seemed to us to be the technically superior hardware. (The Atari 400, with its hard-to-type-on, flat, membrane keyboard, wasn't even considered.) Dad remembers: "You wanted the Atari 800, nothing else. It WAS the sexiest looking computer of all of them." I remember endlessly discussing the possibility of having our own computer and what we might be able to do with one, on the long drives from Agoura to Dad's house and back.

Weeks later, we went together to buy the computer, to Service Merchandise, a strange store that we hadn't been to before. It wasn't really a computer store — they sold everything. There were stacks of soda cans for sale as well as jewelry and electronics. I remember the look on Dad's face when he wrote the check: writing the word "one" then taking a deep breath and giving me a significant look before writing out the next painful word — "thousand." This was a huge amount of money for him, a not-necessary expense for a gadget that neither of us knew exactly what it would do.

When I asked Dad about that day, he told me, "I didn't think we needed a computer and had no idea why we would need one. I kept asking you what we needed it for and you answered, 'We just need it.' I also remember that you were a great at whining. I am glad that you were because you wore me down." (Whining? Clearly I remember those events differently.)

We didn't know it then, but that computer was a great investment, instilling in me a love for computers that would help me create a career as a technology writer, and later another career as an online publisher.

Besides the computer itself, Dad bought a floppy disk drive, a couple of joysticks, and two cartridges: Pac-Man and Atari BASIC. For a monitor, we used a small Trinitron TV that Dad already owned.

When we got it home, it was time to dig in, to unbox that powerful new machine. It was time to … rearrange furniture? In what was certainly the most painful wait in my short life, Dad decided to move the desk around to accommodate the computer and — I don't know, vacuumed the carpet where the desk had moved from, and maybe hand-wrote a few dozen letters and knitted a scarf. I have no idea what he was doing, but it certainly wasn't the most important thing in the world: plugging in the new Atari.

But then, he did.

* * *

That Atari 800 was my first love. I don't mean that figuratively. I loved spending time in front of that machine. Because it was my dad's computer, and because I only saw my dad every other weekend, my time in front of the computer was limited. Dad would pick me up on Saturday morning and drive me to his house at the beach. On Sunday at 5 p.m. Dad would drive me back home to my mom and Joe. In between, I would cram as much time as possible in front of the Atari, sometimes at the expense of time with Dad. But not always — we also spent a lot of time using it together.

A house at the beach might have been a selling point for most boys — they could learn to surf, get a tan, talk to girls. I didn't need those things — there was an Atari indoors. I was simply drawn to that computer. I liked the look of the keyboard, with the lid that popped up to reveal not one but two cartridge slots. No other computer had two cartridge slots. I liked the colorful System Reset, Option, Select, Start buttons, and the fact that it had four game ports. With four ports you could connect four joysticks or eight paddle controllers. I loved the in-store demo program, which played a jaunty little disco tune while the Atari 800 extolled its virtues. There was a lot to love from a technical perspective. Dad's machine had 48KB of RAM. Atari had just started shipping the 800s with that much memory; just a few weeks before, the machine would have come with only 32K. Sure, 48KB wasn't quite as much as the 64KB in the Commodore 64, but the Atari made up for it with a palette of 256 colors (vs. the Commodore's paltry 16) and the best graphics of any computer on the market. It also had the best sound, with the ability to play four notes at a time, edging out the Commodore's three. (Commodore aficionados will argue that the C64's awesome SID music chip was better than my Atari's sound chip. Perhaps, but you can't argue with 11-year-old me.)

The Atari seemed approachable and fun, and I wanted to learn everything I could about it, by sitting in front of the keyboard, reading about it, and being around other people who knew about it.

Dad loved the computer too, and it was an activity that we could do together. We would spend hours playing computer games together — M.U.L.E. and Jumpman were favorites. We would spend hours typing in the BASIC program code for games from computer magazines, and hours more debugging the games when they didn't work the first ten times. Sometimes it was because we had mis-typed the code. It was usually an enjoyable challenge to hunt the bug.

The Atari 800 at
Dad's house.

On the other hand, sometimes it was because the program printed in the magazine wasn't right, meaning we'd have to wait a month or two for the correction to appear in a later issue. We spent hours learning BASIC and then doing little programming projects together.

I didn't let even a minute of potential computer time go to waste. After dinner, Dad and I would watch a bit of TV (maybe The Greatest American Hero or Not Necessarily the News) then I'd go back to the Atari for more of whatever my current project was, usually creating a program in BASIC. Dad would fall asleep in front of the TV, leaving me unfettered access to the computer until the wee hours of the morning. Eventually I'd go to bed, but I'd always be at it again in the morning, before Dad was awake, back to my project at the computer. To Dad, it may have seemed like I never slept at all.

I created many games and utilities in Atari BASIC. My first real program — a thing that I created from scratch that I was really proud of — was a game called Number Flasher. The program flashed a number on the screen for a fraction of a second, then asked you to type the number. It sounds simple (and it was), but this was perhaps the most over-engineered simple BASIC game ever: it included an animated title screen, a choice of difficulty levels, and other useless features that turned what could have been a five-line program into an epic project.

Early on, programming taught me the unexpected lesson that it's possible to solve a problem by not thinking about it. I'd be stuck on a particular dilemma, unsure how to make a program do what I wanted it to do, or with a bug that I didn't know how to fix. I could stare at the cursor for hours, trying in vain to solve the problem in vain. The answer would only come to me at breakfast the next day, or while watching a movie with Dad — the solution would appear when I wasn't actively thinking about the problem. This remains true for me today. Some of my best ideas come when I'm in the shower or just falling asleep. I do my best thinking when I'm not thinking.

I had some failed programming projects, too: a choose-your-own adventure space exploration game that had too many story forks, not enough planning, and got unwieldy. Another uncompleted game let you mix chemicals in a test tube. I still think that idea has potential. When Dad left teaching to manage a travel agency, I tried to create a program to help with the agency's mandatory ticket sales report for the Airline Reporting Commission. That was too big of a project for me, even if I had seven days a week to work on it instead of four days each month.

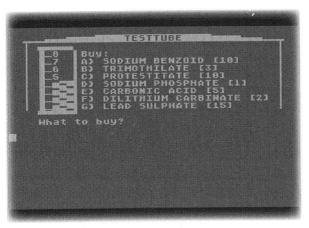

Unfinished Test Tube game.

BASIC allowed me to make the computer do what I wanted, but it had limitations. BASIC was good at doing one thing at a time. The best games that Dad and I played were programmed in assembly language, which could make the machine appear to do several things at once: you could control the thing on the screen, and lots of other things on the screen were also moving, and there was music playing in the background. Assembly language made the Atari walk and chew gum at the same time. With BASIC, I could make the computer walk, or chew the gum, but not both at once. I wanted to eventually learn assembly language, and made a small effort to do so, but it would have required more time than I was able to give it, every other weekend. That achievement, of doing some rudimentary assembly language programming on the Atari, wouldn't come for many years, when I had a wife and a house and my own Atari computer.

ATARI FRIENDS

Many of my friends in middle school also had Atari computers. Once my dad chose the Atari, I naturally gravitated toward kids who also had Atari computers at home: Danny, Marc, Vivek, and Mike. Even though we met when we were maybe 12 years old, I'm still friends with all of those guys today. While they have moved on from their love of their Atari computers, I can't help but feel that our friendship is rooted in that initial bond over the similar hardware that our parents happened to buy. If my dad had bought a Commodore 64 or a TRS-80 instead of that Atari, would I have hung out with a different group of kids in middle school? As a domino effect, would I have a completely different set of friends today, some 30 years later?

The fact that a computer platform could create social groups might seem stupid today. I don't think today's budding geeks divide themselves into Mac and PC factions. Well, maybe they do. But today's computing platforms — Windows, MacOS, and Linux — have more in common than they have differences. The interfaces are similar, their views into the Web are practically identical — heck, each system can even run software for the others pretty well.

In the early days of home computers, each computer system was an island of its own, incompatible with other systems. If you had a Commodore 64 and wanted to trade games, you needed to find the other kid on the playground who also had a C64 ... because the kid with the Atari (or even the Commodore VIC-20) was useless to you as a game trader. And if you were learning to program your computer — well, all the machines could be programmed in BASIC, but each platform understood its own dialect, so your awesome BASIC programming tricks for your Apple // were worthless on my Atari. So it makes sense that social groups and friendships could form based on something as a random as what brand of gadget our parents brought home.

Despite the fact that Commodore 64 was the best-selling computer at the time, I barely used them and barely knew the kids who might have had them. The same effect was in play in video gaming: the Atari 2600 was by far the most popular game system. Yes, a few of my friends had one and I played it when I had the opportunity, but overall I spent very little time playing one: when it came to video games, I was an Intellivision kid.

My Atari friends were smart and competitive, although maybe not the best at following through on projects. Once, Vivek and I made a bet about which of us would write a book first. He was working on a fantasy novel. I was working with Danny on a humorous sci-fi story about a hapless man who won the deed to a space casino in a card game. Danny and I didn't get past chapter two. I don't know how far Vivek made it on his book, but I did win the bet ten years later when I wrote my first book about the Internet. In another competition that never went anywhere, my friends wagered on who could publish an Atari game first. Marc and I worked on DungeonQuest, which would have been a Dungeons and Dragons-type adventure. We only managed to create an awesome, almost-working title screen. Our competition, Vivek and Mike, didn't finish their game either — so I guess the jury is still out on that bet.

SOFTWARE PIRACY

When Dad first got the Atari, we didn't have much software for it: the Pac-Man cartridge, the BASIC cart, and whatever BASIC programs we typed in ourselves from the manuals and magazines. In sixth grade, I met some older boys in the locker room who also used an Atari, and they were willing to get me copies of games for the price of $1 per game. (Finally! P.E. class was good for something.) Every couple of weeks, I would meet these two guys and buy a disk of five games for $5. I would have to wait agonizing days until it was my weekend to visit Dad, and we'd see what was on the disk.

I would request games that I'd heard of, and sometimes my locker room source would be able to provide those games. Other times, I just got what I got. Sometimes one or more of the games didn't work. Maybe they didn't copy over correctly or they were just bum files. Sorry, kid, there are no refunds in the mean world of boys' locker room software piracy. You pay your money, you take your chances.

I don't remember those characters' names. They weren't friends; this was strictly business. I don't even think either of them had an Atari of their own: they were using someone else's machine to copy games for me. Occasionally the drop went bad — the sellers didn't show up at the agreed-upon day and time, and Dad and I would have to suffer two weeks without a fresh stash of games. Sometimes I didn't have $5, and again we would have to go without.

Luckily, this arrangement didn't need to last long. My friends at school who had Ataris of their own eventually made their own connections and started getting software to trade.

Software piracy was the norm for us. All the computer kids I knew did it. We were children; we couldn't afford to buy games and other software. We called it "trading." It was incredibly easy to copy games from one disk to another. Other people (no one I knew) did the hard work of removing the copy protection from the original software. By the time we got the software, making a copy for a friend took no technical skill.

Eventually Dad and I had many disks with several games on each. We had disk cases — the kind that would hold 50 floppies, or 70 if you really crammed them in — filled with disks. I created an alphabetized list of the games, cross-indexed with the code number of the disk it was on. The list went on for pages and pages and pages of fanfold computer paper. Master of the Lamps was on disk 52; The Apshai Trilogy on disk 117. (I don't have that list anymore; wish I did. I still have most of the disks, but some of them don't work anymore. The data on floppies doesn't last forever.)

Copying games didn't hurt anyone, at least no one we could see. Rampant software piracy probably did hurt the early computing industry somewhat, the industry that created the games that we loved to play. But despite 27 years of propaganda by the Software Publishers Association, I'm still not so sure. The SPA (now called the Software and Information Industry Association) is a trade group that lobbied on behalf of software publishers, trying to convince us all not to pirate software. If you've seen the horrifying '80s rap video "Don't Copy That Floppy" on YouTube, you're already familiar with their work.

I felt conflicted about the situation. In computer magazines, editorials and letters to the editor debated the issue of software piracy. On one hand, I knew using software that we hadn't paid for was wrong. On the other hand, we didn't actually use a lot of the software the we traded. Part of trading programs was simply collecting, being able to boast that you had a large stash of games. After acquiring a new program, we would eagerly try it out — but the ones that were uninteresting, we never used again. Having piles of pirated software seemed like a victimless crime if you never used most of that software.

So as a high school freshman, with this conflict on my mind, I tried to convince my friends that piracy was killing the Atari, that software companies were going to stop supporting the Atari because they couldn't sell enough software. I told them that we should stop pirating games. I didn't convince them — maybe because I wasn't 100 percent convinced myself. (I certainly hadn't stopped copying games.) I wanted to do the right thing, but that was difficult. So I tried to convince my friends to join with me. My friends laughed at the idea. To stop getting free, awesome games for our computers was preposterous. It wasn't long before I stopped my campaign to reform my friends.

A few weeks after I started my no-trading campaign, the new issue of A.N.A.L.O.G. magazine came out. A.N.A.L.O.G. was one of the most popular magazines dedicated to the Atari computers. My best friend Marc had a subscription, and he showed me a letter that was printed in the February 1986 issue:

> *I have read and reread the views on illegal software piracy by many well-known Atari programmers, including Alex Leavens and Russ Wetmore, and I feel that they are approaching the problem from the wrong direction. They seem to think that these pirates copy software because: they don't want to buy it; it's too expensive; or some other lame excuse. Well, I've seen piracy going on all around me, and I can now see that these fools come in two types:*
>
> *(1) The first group (the majority) copy software for the heck of it. They don't try to come up with an excuse, they just do it. Since they have the means to illegally duplicate software, they will continue to do so — and nothing will stop them. If software developers distributed their products on nonprotected disks for $1.98, the problem would still continue. Of course, this "hobby" is illegal. Try to tell them that. All they do is laugh or say, "Who cares?" The part I hate the most is that they enjoy being referred to as "pirates." I've heard many a person brag that he's a pirate, with a couple hundred*

pirated games. It would sound far worse to say, "Hey.
I'm a violator of the United States Copyright Act, which
just happens to be a federal offense requiring five to
ten years in the slammer and up to a $50,000 fine."
So let's toss out the term "pirate." How about using
"illegal software distributor" instead?

(2) The second group is not as big as the first, but is
growing at an incredible rate. This is the group that is
being influenced by the first group. It works like this: so
many people have come in contact with illegally copied
software that it has become part of owning a computer.
I have not met one single computer owner who doesn't
own any illegally obtained software. Not one. The
saddest part of the whole mess is that the majority of
these people do not realize that what they are doing is
illegal. I have seen 3rd graders, housewives, and other
everyday people becoming involved. We are bringing
up a new generation of these people, and nothing is
being done to prevent it. ...

The letter was unsigned. Marc and my other friends
were convinced that I had written it. I tried in vain to convince them that I was a reformed anti-piracy advocate, that
the letter was not written by me. They never believed me.
They teased me mercilessly, for thinking for a moment that
we should do the right thing.

It's an interesting letter from a historical perspective,
because people still share copyrighted material for the
heck of it. They find ways to steal $1.99 iPhone games, as

well as content with no cash value whatsoever, such as TV shows on The Pirate Bay, lovingly digitized and available for download just moments after they are broadcast.

The best part is that today, Marc is an attorney for a big-time Los Angeles law firm that specializes in big-name video game companies. He probably spends his days making pirates' and Pirate Bay downloaders' lives uncomfortable. Maybe *he* wrote that letter.

MODEM

After a year or so with the Atari, Dad decided to get a modem. For readers not born in ye olden days of yore: a modem was a gadget that let your computer connect to another computer using a phone line, like in the movie War Games. You haven't seen War Games? Put this book down now and watch it.

He bought an MPP 1000C modem, a blue plastic box that plugged into the computer's joystick port. Most modems of the day, like the popular (but relatively expensive) Hayes Smartmodem, plugged into the computer's serial port. But the Atari didn't have a standard RS-232 serial port: to get one, you needed to buy yet another expensive piece of hardware. Dad's MPP modem worked around the whole serial port mess by pretending to be a joystick, a slower device that didn't need a serial port. On the upside, it was cheap.

There was a tradeoff, however. It worked at 300 bits per second, which works out to 30 characters per second. You can read faster than 30 characters a second. My friend Vivek had the latest Hayes modem: at 1200 bits per second it was four times faster than Dad's blue modem. At the risk of sounding like an old man shaking my cane in the air and saying, "You darn kids don't know how good you have it! Back in my day ..." I'll just say 300 bits per second was slow. Now get off my lawn.

That modem opened up a new world to us: BBSes. Bulletin Board Systems were small communities that you could dial into. Each BBS offered different features, but typically you could read and write messages in a message board, download files, and play games. If you called a multi-line BBS (which were relatively rare) you could "chat" by typing with the other users who were dialed in at the same time. It seemed amazing to me, that the world of my computer could expand to get the information on computers elsewhere. That far-away machine could cause words and graphics to appear on my screen; it could make my computer beep. Likewise, I could control that far-away machine.

The Atari BBSes in Dad's area, the 213 area code, allowed just one user at a time. If someone else was already calling in when you tried to connect, you got a busy signal and tried again. My favorite BBS was called Weird City. The sysop (system operator, the owner of the BBS) called himself Mayor Finchley, and over time the honorable mayor created a highly customized BBS complete with unique games and a fun community. When we first joined, Weird City was running basic BBS software that didn't even have user accounts or passwords. Finchley worked hard on the software, and eventually there was a downloadable information library, a graphical poker game, and other fun stuff you couldn't find anywhere else.

In real life, Mayor Finchley was a filmmaker named Stanley Sheff. He directed a science fiction movie called Lobster Man From Mars. In 1989, because Dad and I had gotten to know him well on Weird City, Sheff invited us to the premiere. It was at a movie studio lot, where I got to meet Weird Al Yankovic, one of my favorite musicians.

I liked programming the computer, but access to BBSes gave me something new: the ability to share my creations with other people. I wrote several games for Weird City, which could be played by the board's other users. Because Weird City ran on an Atari, it was easy to write programs on my computer that would work on the BBS. Having an audience encouraged me to step up my programming: I created a TV game-show knockoff called Hubcap of Fortune, a first-person explore-the-maze game from the perspective of a rat in the maze, and a text adventure game with a scavenger hunt theme.

There were lots of other BBSes to call. When I found lists of BBSes, which were published in magazines and on other BBSes, I would pore over them looking for new boards. New BBSes would crop up from time to time. Occasionally, a favorite BSS would disappear with little or no notice, when the sysop's computer died, or — if the BBS was run by a kid — the parents took away computer privileges. If a BBS had hours posted, for instance 8 p.m. to 7 a.m., it was a sure sign that it was run by a kid, sharing the home phone line when Mom and Dad didn't need it. It was also a good sign that that board wouldn't have longevity.

A BBS junkie had to be careful. I could only dial in to BBSes that were a local phone call — a certain distance from Dad's house in Playa Del Rey. Beyond the local calling zone were toll calls, which had a per-minute charge. I had to be especially wary, because the 213 area code included plenty of toll prefixes as well as local prefixes. Phone numbers beyond the toll calling zone were long-distance: more expensive still. I needed to stick with the free-to-call local BBSes.

Computing platform also limited the range of BBSes I would call. For the most part, I only called into BBSes that ran on Atari computers. Sure, there were BBSes that ran on Apple //s, Commodore 64s, and IBM PCs, which my Atari could dial into. But a loyal Atari user wouldn't want to venture into those neighborhoods too often. First of all, due to the Atari-only ATASCII character set, Atari BBSes looked best for callers who also had Atari computers. Any software that was available for download on those other systems wouldn't work on my Atari. So that left the community aspect, the message boards themselves. The problem there was, the message boards were full of loyal Apple // or Commodore 64 or whatever users — if they found out that you owned an Atari, the conversation would devolve into arguments about why Atari computers sucked so hard.

Most BBSes offered software to download: they were an effective (though not particularly fast) way to get new games and utilities for your machine. If a BBS offered pirated software for download, it was called a warez board. If it didn't, there still might be stuff worth downloading: there were all sorts of fun public domain games, applications someone typed in from magazines, and shareware. (Shareware was software that was free to use, but you were expected or encouraged to pay something if you liked it.) Some BBSes claimed to be warez-free, but if the sysop trusted you, you could be granted access to the secret inner circle, the warez levels.

Many BBSes, but all of those that offered warez, had strict rules about how much you could download. The sysop didn't want leeches tying up the phone line all day and night, downloading every game in the library. So download/upload ratios were enforced: for instance, you had to upload 1KB of new software for every 2KB that you downloaded.

I also discovered the ability to create images and simple animations using the Atari's special character set. I started creating some of these online cartoons for Weird City and other local BBSes. In retrospect, some of them were pretty good and I'm proud of them. Others weren't so good. I enjoyed creating these comics; I started using the moniker Kevin Komix on the BBSes. I created a monthly cartoon for Weird City, and animated login pages for several other bulletin boards.

At first, I used a program called LeBreak to create the pages of graphics, but LeBreak had one annoying trait that

I hated: every time you hit the backspace key, it would clear the screen and re-render your graphic from the very beginning, leaving off the last character that you typed. Wasn't it possible to just delete the last character without waiting while the computer re-drew the animation? So I set out to build a better mousetrap, which I called the Kevin Komix Kartoon Kreator.

After I developed the KKKK program I distributed it to several local BBSes, and I imagine that it was used by tens of people. Or maybe closer to ten. A friend used it to create graphics for a TV station where he was an intern. I eventually created three versions. Version 3 of the program included several built-in fonts that I designed: you could type a phrase and it would render your message in big letters in the font of your choice. There was a search-and-replace feature. It's hard to believe, but those little things were a big deal and as far as I knew, mine was the only ATASCII art software that did all of those things, plus the time-saving backspace feature that was my reason for creating it in the first place.

Another of my favorite BBSes was The Kitchen, which had a system operator who called himself Melted Butter. For that board, I created a kitchen-themed kartoon for every day of the week, which users would see when they logged in. I created login screens and kartoons for many

BBSes — I was getting my first taste of getting my work published online (which apparently I liked because I've stuck with it in my work).

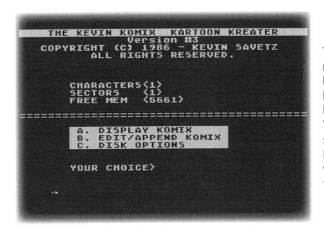

The main menu of the Kevin Komix Kartoon Kreator. Yikes, I spelled Kreator wrong on the top line.

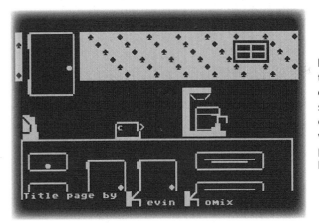

I created this kitchen cabinet scene, complete with coffee pot, for The Kitchen BBS.

43

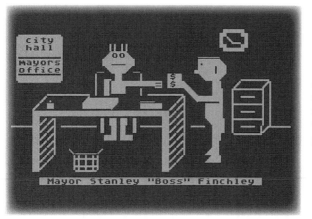

A citizen gives the mayor of Weird City a bribe.

Another service to call — it wasn't exactly a bulletin board — was called Buy Phone. It was an online yellow pages and classified ads service. It was pretty much a miniature Craigslist, in 1987. The only interesting thing about Buy Phone was that through it I met a kid named Tim, who ended up being one of my best friends for many years. We would visit each others' houses to trade games and play M.U.L.E.

M.U.L.E.

My top two favorite favorite games on the Atari 800 were (and remain) Jumpman and M.U.L.E. Dad and I played those games endlessly. The games couldn't be more different — Jumpman is a jump-and-run game; M.U.L.E. a supply/demand and economics simulation.

M.U.L.E. — all those periods sure make it tedious to type — stands for Multi Use Labor Element. I know; it sounds so thrilling. Supply and demand! Arcane acronyms!

The plot of the game is this: colonists land on a new planet, where they must stake out plots of land and then grow the elements necessary to survive on the planet: food, energy, and Smithore, from which M.U.L.E.s are constructed. If you don't have enough of something, you can buy it from another player or the store. If you have an abundance, you can sell it. In the standard game you have 12 rounds, representing one year, to create a thriving colony. M.U.L.E. offered a combination of competition and collaboration that was rare in games. You could earn a lot of money at the expense of other players by cornering the market on Smithore, but what's the point if the colony as a whole doesn't survive?

Two other things make M.U.L.E. an exceptional game: the ability to have four players, and the computer players' artificial intelligence. Unlike many games that required just one or exactly two players, M.U.L.E. allows from one player (who'd play against three computer opponents), up

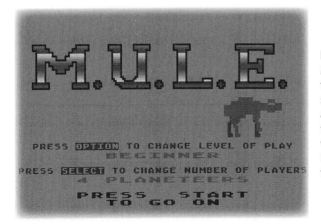

I started M.U.L.E. just to get this screenshot, and now the theme song will be stuck in my head for days.

to four human players. Most of the time, Dad and I would play together against two computer players, which never got dull. The game seemed to have a variety of personalities for the computer opponents: some were team players, some were not. Some had a tendency to hoard one element or another.

Although the in-game artificial intelligence was pretty impressive for the era, the best games — though rare for us — were the ones where we managed to get four humans together. Today the idea of four gamers playing together is dwarfed by what's possible with massively multiplayer online games ... but this was more of a precursor to a good old-fashioned LAN party, where friends bring their computers one place, connect them, and play together and trash-talk. I'd play four-way M.U.L.E. with my school friends Marc, Danny, Mike, and Vivek on weekends and sleepovers.

As an aside, at a World Of Atari convention with Dad, circa 1988 in the L.A. area, I got my first experience with a real LAN party. "MIDI Maze" was a first-person shooter played on 16 (wow!) Atari ST computers. Players, represented by Have A Nice Day-style smiley faces, would stalk around a 3D maze shooting one another, deathmatch style. The game's programmers (ab)used the ST's Musical Instrument Digital Interface (MIDI) connection — meant for controlling synthesizers and the like — to get that many Ataris networked together. I loved the idea of connecting that many computers, but the game itself was interesting to me for only a few minutes. It would be a few years before

Doom really popularized the first-person shooter genre, and with it, the word "frag." I'm pretty sure at that convention center in 1988, I was ahead of the curve. I got fragged hard.

Back to M.U.L.E. The game was tied together by a catchy theme song, a rockin' tune in four-part-harmony that could lodge itself in your brain for days. The modern chiptune band "8 Bit Weapon" does a nice version the M.U.L.E. theme song, which you can get here: www.8bitweapon .com/music.htm.

I liked M.U.L.E. so much that I wrote a letter to Dan Bunten, the creator of the game. I told him how much I enjoyed the game, how much fun I had playing with my dad and friends.

I felt sort of guilty at the time I wrote the letter, and I feel sort of guilty now, that we never actually purchased the game. My dad and I — and I assume, all of my friends — all played pirated copies of M.U.L.E.

To my utter delight, Dan wrote back to me. He told me that he didn't get much fan mail, but he was happy that I enjoyed M.U.L.E. I wrote back to Dan, trying to establish a regular communication, but didn't hear from him again. After a few weeks I wrote to him again, but didn't get another reply. I was disappointed.

Many, many years later, I learned that Dan changed genders in the early 1990s (she called it her "pronoun change" and changed her name to Danielle) and died in 1998. I had no idea then, and equally have no idea now, what Dan might have been going through while high-school Kevin was trying to strike up a pen-pal friendship.

He probably had more important things to think about when I was writing to him in the late 1980s.

I love this quote from Danielle, and think of it often: "No one ever said on their deathbed, 'Gee, I wish I had spent more time alone with my computer.'"

M.U.L.E. was also available for the Commodore 64 (a version that I never played), the Apple //, and the Nintendo Entertainment System, a darn good implementation. Wikipedia says it was also available for several other weird systems (MSX-2, PC-8801 MKII, and Sharp X1) but who knows; you can't believe everything you read on the Internet. Today, there's a pretty great Internet version of M.U.L.E. that remains true to the original gameplay. The graphics are improved, but the catchy theme song remains. It's free, available for Mac, Windows, and Linux, at www.planetmule.com.

CHAPTER 4
MIDDLE SCHOOL

The Atari 800 was my first love, but with every-other-weekend visitation, I had limited access to it. So I cheated on it with other computing platforms. When I reached A.E. Wright Middle School, which spanned sixth through eighth grades, I gained access to other kinds of computers.

Even before I touched it, the TRS-80 Model III looked like a very different sort of computer than my beloved Atari. Its one-piece silver molded case included the keyboard, monitor, and space for two floppy disk drives — a very different look than the Atari's external drives and TV monitor for the display. When I sat down at it, other differences were quickly apparent: the screen didn't have color — just white letters on a black background — and there was no sound at all. But the machines were littered around A.E. Wright Middle School, and they were oddly appealing. Those one-piece silver cases looked futuristic, even though the technology inside seemed less advanced than the Atari.

TRS-80s were only sold at Radio Shack stores. (The TRS stood for Tandy Radio Shack.) We little geeky kids called it "Trash 80," and its companion printer, the DMP-100, "Dump 100." For 11-year-old boys, this was comedy gold that wrote itself. Why did Radio Shack's marketing department make it so easy for us?

Like most computers, the TRS-80 used the BASIC programming language. The computer that I learned to program on lived in the library behind the librarian's desk. Another kid showed me how to put a line number followed by the command PRINT and some text in quotes. When I typed RUN, the computer obediently printed those words back on the screen.

That first time with TRS-80 BASIC, I had a game in mind, a sort of adventure game that I called Desert Google, which had something do with with exploring the desert on a camel. I opened the manual that lived in the drawer next to the computer, and learned what I needed to know, the moment that I needed to know it: like how to let the player type something (INPUT A$), and how to do something different based on what the player typed (IF ... THEN). I spent countless hours in front of that library computer.

The Trash 80 in the library had a disk drive, but for my first few weeks of using it, I didn't have a floppy disk, therefore no way to save the program I was creating. So, for several days every time I sat down at the computer before school or during lunch period, I would start to type the game from scratch, from memory. As a result, the game never got very long, and I never completed it. Still, Desert Google provided my halting first steps into programming.

Accessing that computer in the library was tricky. First, the librarian had priority. She used it for keeping track of overdue books and other library chores. When the librarian had information to enter about book checkouts, sometimes I'd do her data entry, so eager was I to have access to the machine. If she wasn't using it, kids could sign up on a first-come, first-served basis. Not that there were a lot of proto-geeks competing for the library's computer, but there was some competition for that spot. A maximum of two kids could use the computer at a time.

Soon I acquired a floppy disk. My time in the glow of the library's computer was spent exploring the operating system, typing and playing simple games from magazines and books, and playing some commercial games. Someone brought me a copy of Telengard, a dungeon exploration game that helped lay the foundation for dozens of computer games since, including Rogue and Nethack.

During a trip to Radio Shack, I invested some birthday money in XENOS, a text adventure game about an alien invasion in the desert (I'm pretty sure it takes place in a different desert than Desert Google). I didn't finish the game, but it's not too late. I still have the diskette … and it's possible to download the game along with a TRS-80 emulator.

I wrote a program for the school's open house night, which displayed a couple of pictures in the TRS-80's low-resolution graphics. I worked on that program for days during lunch periods, and was incredibly proud when the librarian moved the computer to a more visible spot on her desk and let my program run for parents to see.

After a while, I learned that the TRS-80 in the library wasn't the only computer on campus. In fact, there were a lot of computers on campus, all TRS-80s. On the edge of campus there were the "R buildings," a huddle of portable, "temporary" buildings (temporary in name only — they must have been in that spot for more than a decade). In one of them there was a lab full of Model IIIs, which were used primarily for torturously boring math drills.

To keep the computers inexpensive, the lab computers didn't have disk drives: they were fed programs over slow cassette interfaces which were connected to a master computer in the lab. Initially, all 15 "slave" computers could be fed a program — e.g. Boring Math Drills for Kids — at the same time. It took awhile to send the program over the cassette interface, but because they all received the program simultaneously, each computer would be ready to run the program at the same time. The system could also send a program to a single computer at a time. When the math drill became intolerable, a kid could "accidentally" press the orange reset button on his or her TRS-80, nuking the program from memory and earning the kid a five-minute break while the teacher re-sent the program to that computer.

The math teacher, Mr. Rosensweig, had a TRS-80 in his classroom. I was in his class one year, but I was terrible at math, and didn't pay too much attention to his lessons, so as a result he didn't like me. There was no way he was going to let me use his computer. There were a couple more computers in the school office, but kids weren't welcome in there. We only ventured to the office for talks with the vice principal, which no one wanted. Sigh. More TRS-80s that I would never get to explore.

In seventh and eighth grade, I discovered journalism class. I loved writing for the school newspaper. I loved the teacher, Mrs. Hartman. As a bonus, Mrs. Hartman's classroom was in the R buildings, right next to the computer lab. I could use the computers as needed for my hard-hitting journalism. One of my published articles was an interview with a teacher's dog.

In my third and final year at A.E. Wright, eighth grade, another lab appeared in the center of campus, filled with TRS-80 model IIIs and the gleaming white (not silver) new model IV machines. I wanted in there badly. But it wasn't open to students, at least not on an ad-hoc basis. Maybe it was only open to certain classes at designated times. Maybe it wouldn't be open until the next year, when I had moved on to high school. All I know is that it wasn't open TO ME. It was terribly unfair, all of those shiny white computers sitting idle.

As part of a class project in eighth grade, I tried to start a computer club on campus — one in which we would have sanctioned access to the computer labs after school and during breaks, and BASIC programming classes. I wanted to give it the high-tech name COMP-U-WRIGHT. I was blown off by the administration; told they had plans to do that next year. Great, but next year I wouldn't be there. I'd be in high school.

Thinking back on it, I wonder where the money came from for all of those computers at that school. We were in a fairly well-to-do area, but it wasn't Beverly Hills either. Where did the cash for two labs of computers, plus various other machines scattered around campus, come from? And although there were plenty of computers on campus, it seemed like the administration didn't want the kids actually touching them too much, getting our grubby hands on their expensive machines.

SIXTH GRADE: YIKES!

1982 and 1983, when I was in sixth grade, was an eventful time. That school year, I had a major health issue: papilledema, or intercranial swelling that put too much pressure on my optic nerve. I had a constant headache for months, and spent a total of one month, in three installments, at Cedars Sinai hospital. For a while the doctors thought I had a brain tumor (I didn't) and that I might go blind (I didn't do that either.)

The headache was bad, but the effects of the treatment made me pretty miserable: I had to take steroids, which made me, the skinniest skinny kid ever, plump up like a balloon. The upside was that I got to get out of P.E. class a lot — not because I couldn't participate for health reasons, but because my awesome neurologist understood that I hated P.E. and wrote me a note to get out of it. (I spent some of that P.E. time in the library playing with the computer.)

Also, to help me cope, Mom and Joe probably bought me more Intellivision games than I deserved. It's easy to make light of it now, but then the situation was stressful for my whole family, plus incredibly expensive. A month in the hospital isn't cheap.

There was a man at the hospital whose job it was to make sure kids were happy during their stay. On the day I arrived he gave me a Super Simon toy to keep. (Simon, in case you missed that cultural phenomena, was an electronic memory game: colored lights would alight in a particular order, with accompanying musical tones, then the player tried to press the lights in the same order.) There was an Atari 2600 with a TV on a cart that could be rolled from room to room. When I was feeling well enough, I played a lot of Missile Command with the other sick kids. (You could also get a TV with a VCR brought to your room. The only movie I remember watching on it was An Officer and A Gentleman, which my mom wanted to see. The most boring movie ever made — so says 12-year-old me. Maybe it's actually great; I haven't watched it since.)

By the time the school year was over, the papilledema problem was over too. The doctors didn't know why it started, and they didn't know why it finally went away. Dad took me on a big trip during summer vacation: we flew to London, then went on a tour to Spain, Portugal, and Morocco. It was an incredible and memorable trip. We saw and did and ate amazing things. But for geeky young Kevin, it was hard to be away from computers for three weeks. I brought a notepad with me, and spent downtime in the hotel writing programs in BASIC, in my notepad … to be typed into the Atari 800 when we got back home.

One of our hotels in Spain had a slot machine in the lobby, and there I had my first experience gambling. In Spain at the time, the guideline for drinking alcohol was: if you're old enough to hold a glass, you're old enough to drink. I didn't drink anything other than Coke, but the rules for using the slot machine were apparently something similar.

The slot machine in the hotel would let you drop in some pesetas, spin the reels, then there was a feature where you could lock one or two of the reels in place, then spin the remaining reels again. I don't know if the machine was broken, if I was gifted at picking the right reels to lock, or if I was just lucky, but I won a good amount of money that day in the hotel lobby, maybe $100. The next day, Dad and I went to an electronics shop in Madrid where I bought a Nintendo Game & Watch "Mario Bros." game (which I still have) — and had cash left over.

JUMPMAN

That leftover cash, plus my Dad's end-of-summer birthday, led me to discover one of my all-time favorite Atari 800 games — Jumpman.

Jumpman was one of the few commercial games that I actually bought rather than acquired via trading or downloading. With the leftover money from the Europe trip — I guess I didn't buy enough souvenirs — I walked into a computer store and asked about new games for the Atari. The clerk handed me Jumpman and told me what a fantastic game it was and how much he loved it. It didn't look like much — the black-and-white screenshot on the back of the box wasn't too impressive, but based on the clerk's glowing recommendation, I paid the money and wrapped it up for Dad, never having played it.

I gave the game to Dad, and we had a great time that weekend playing and playing it. In the game, you're this running-jumping guy who needs to collect all the bombs (which look like peanuts, so everyone called them peanuts) from each level of a building. The nifty thing is that each level is unique, with its own baddies to avoid, who behave differently than all the other baddies on the other levels. For instance, one level had stupid robots that followed a simple path. Another had smart robots that would stalk you mercilessly. One level had cute little dragons to shoot, another had bombs that dropped relentlessly from the top of the screen. Some of the levels are puzzles — for instance, the peanuts need to be picked up in the proper order, or

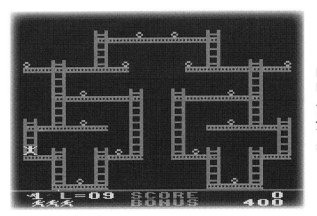

I lost three lives in Jumpman just taking this screenshot.

else. One particularly sneaky puzzle level had yet another level hidden within it. That was the only level that I never fully solved — the game was designed to show you that level relatively rarely, so figuring it out was an extra challenge. Of course, the solution is available on the Web now. You couldn't Google the spoilers back then.

The game's weakness was a level called Mystery Maze, in which the whole playfield is blacked out. Unable to see where you're going, you've got to move the guy with special care, and it takes forever. Most levels take a minute or less for an experienced player — Mystery Maze would take 10 or 15. Sometimes randomly landing on that level, I'd just smash the restart button and give up on the game in progress. I wished someone would create a hacked version that excluded that level, but to my knowledge no one did.

Later, they came out with Jumpman Junior, which had all new levels. Although the game had fewer levels than the original, it was more difficult because you couldn't see a level unless you finished all the levels before it. So by the time I reached a new level, I didn't have many lives left to experiment with the new level, and losing meant playing though from the start again. Too frustrating for me. As a result, although I finished Jumpman many times, I don't think I've seen the higher levels of Junior.

As an adult, I've played the Commodore 64 version of Jumpman, and I love that many of the levels are completely different from the ones on the Atari version. I suspect the gameplay differences are because of technical differences between the machines: some programming tricks that were trivial on the Atari might be almost impossible on the C64, and vice versa. Regardless, it's like a whole new set of levels to complete: awesome. I just played the Apple // version for the first time in an emulator. It's terrible. The Apple's graphics and sound just aren't up to that challenge. Similarly, Wikipedia says there was also an IBM PC version — I'm frightened by my mental estimate of how bad it must be.

You can play the original, not terrible, Jumpman on an Atari or C64 emulator. There are also a variety of more modern, but similar games. On Windows, I like Hap Hazard (www.raptisoft.com/haphazard) and I've heard good things about Jumpman Zero (www.jumpmanzero.com). For the Mac, I don't know of anything new, but emulators work fine for the original thing.

(Here's the type of super-extra-geeky detail that interests me. Feel free to disagree.) Speaking of emulators: on Jumpman's attract screen — the level it shows while it's waiting for a player to start the game — the guy runs, climbs, and jumps in a pre-programmed path around a level that, oddly, doesn't appear in the actual game. As a kid, I always wished there was a way to play that level. As an adult, playing Jumpman on an Atari emulator on my Mac, I discovered that the attract screen level is governed by the game's physics engine — it's not just a pre-recorded animation, which might have been easier to program. Most emulators have an option that forces the emulated computer to run at the speed of the original machine — which makes games work at the speed that they're supposed to. I found that if you turn off that speed limitation, allowing the emulated Atari to run at speeds impossible for real Atari hardware, the timing would be wrong for the running-climbing-jumping of the attract screen. The little guy would jump at the wrong time, crash his way to the bottom of the screen, and die on the demo level. I might have been the first person to see that bug in action.

Back to 1983. A couple of months after buying Jumpman, I was back in that computer store. I saw the same clerk and thanked him for recommending Jumpman. I started talking about some aspect of the game and he stopped me, uninterested — "I've never played it." Damn. I learned a lesson about sales that day.

LODE RUNNER

Of course, my friends and I played lots and lots of other games on the Atari. My friend Mike wanted to get the best score on Track and Field. In that game, you control a runner on a racetrack. The faster you wiggle the joystick back and forth, the faster your runner will run — simple. But try as you might, there's a limit to how fast the human hand can wiggle a joystick. So Mike attached a handheld sander to his joystick. It turns out that the power tool, meant to shake a piece of sandpaper back and forth at high speed, will also shake a joystick back and forth at high speed. The Track and Field runner practically flew off of the screen, finishing the race in record time. Of course, that was a trick you could do only once — that race destroyed Mike's joystick.

Lode Runner is a more sedate game.

In Lode Runner, you control a little dude who runs across brick platforms, climbs up and down ladders, and collects gold bars. Meanwhile, stupid-but-deadly guards try to get you. You've got a gun, but in a twist that was unprecedented (and may remain unique), you don't use the gun to shoot the guards. Instead, you shoot the ground, creating holes in the floor that you can fall through to safety, or that the guards can get stuck in.

Although they are both essentially platformers — games in which you run and jump around platforms and obstacles — the gameplay of Lode Runner and Jumpman are very different. Lode Runner can fall and fall without dying, but a fall of a moderate distance means death for Jumpman. Jumpman can jump (thanks, Dr. Obvious); Lode Runner can't. Imagine the hilarity that ensues when switching from one game to the other, forgetting which laws of physics your little running guy lives under. This has caused many senseless pixelated deaths.

I didn't love Lode Runner back in the day — it was OK. I appreciate it more now. Some cool things about Lode Runner: first, there are 150 levels. The rules and bad guys are exactly the same for every level — no new concepts or items are revealed as you progress. So while the game lacks the variety of Jumpman, 150 levels does give a game a whole lot of replay value. Plus, there is a level editor, allowing players to build their own playfields. I guarantee that every kid who ever played Lode Runner built a level that spelled out their name in bricks and ladders.

Dad bought Lode Runner at the Egghead Software store (located on Pico Boulevard between Bundy and Barrington. Why do I remember that? I couldn't even drive then. I bet I can put that brain cell to better use.) Dad and I would often stop at that store on the Saturday morning drive from my house to his. It was exciting to see the software and hardware on display — the store was always crowded with customers.

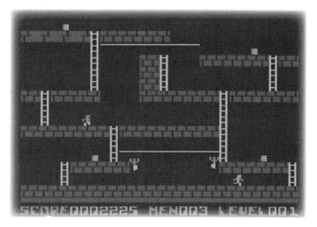

Lode Runner.

Lode Runner was available for many computer systems, and is implemented equally well on all of them that I've tried. My friend Adam had an Apple //, and Lode Runner was just as smooth-playing and fun on the Apple as it was on the Atari.

Adam was my friend until the seventh grade "Medieval Market," when we had a disagreement about the amount of space required for our shield and swords booth ... then he wasn't my friend anymore. My mom has a picture of us arguing that day, standing in a schoolyard surrounded by Joe's collection of swords and spiked shields. I can't believe they let me bring real swords and spiked shields onto a school playground. That sure wouldn't fly today.

TI 99/4A

Soon, I would have a computer of my own, in my room. One which I could use every day instead of every other weekend. Unfortunately, the way I got it was not honorable. I stole it. I stole it in front of hundreds of people.

My mom worked as the office manager at a Catholic church. She started there when I was in kindergarten and worked there until after I graduated from college. She was a central part of the activity at St. Jude's, and everyone knew her. I was there a lot, too — hanging around her office and the rectory in the summer, on sick days from school, and so on. All the church people knew me. We went to mass every Sunday, and I went to CCD (religious education class) every Tuesday after school. (I must have missed the day they taught "thou shalt not steal.")

Every October, the church would have a big fundraiser called Octoberfest. Held in the parking lot, there were rides, games, carnival booths, a cake walk, and other family fun. A raffle always closed out the day. The raffle was a big moneymaker for the church's facility improvement projects, and raffle ticket sales started months before the Octoberfest carnival day. The staff and volunteers (including myself, sometimes) would mail thousands of envelopes containing raffle tickets to parishioners, who would hopefully mail back their signed raffle tickets plus a check. All of the purchased tickets would be thrown into a large spinning bin. It had mesh walls, so you could spin the bin and watch thousands of the paper tickets climb, fall, and tumble around and around.

By the time Octoberfest rolled around, the bin was stuffed with tickets. The prizes were pretty great: the grand prize was usually a trip to Hawaii. Although it varied from year to year, other prizes included things like a car, a vacation condo for a week, $500 cash, Walkman radios ... and in that particular October of 1982, a Texas Instruments 99/4A computer.

I wanted that computer. Well, no. I wanted an Atari of my own like at Dad's house, but failing that, I wanted any computer. The TI, with the colorful graphics on the box, seemed like a good alternative. I saw that box a lot in the weeks preceding the raffle — it was in the rectory, part of the stack of raffle prizes stored in Mom's office.

I had already tried traditional methods of getting a computer — asking my parents for one again and again. That wasn't working. Saving up for one myself must have seemed like an insurmountable task. I even went to reality TV for help in my quest to get a computer of my own.

From one TV season in 1982 to 1983, NBC aired a show called Fantasy, in which "ordinary people from all over the United States would write in to have their wishes granted on national television," so says IMDb. One summer day, Mom took me to sit in the studio audience for a taping of Fantasy. (Living in Southern California's San

Fernando Valley, it was pretty easy to pop over the hill to Hollywood to see tapings at CBS Television City or Universal Studios.)

While the group of audience members was standing in line, waiting to be let into the studio, we were asked to fill out sheets describing our own fantasy. (If I recall correctly, some audience members' fantasies were granted as part of the show.) I filled out the form, requesting an Atari 800 computer with an 810 disk drive, and probably whatever other peripherals and add-ons I could cram onto the little piece of paper. Where the form asked why I deserved to have my fantasy fulfilled, I wrote: because I had been sick. Mom filled out a form, too, requesting "a computer" for me, and going into a little more detail about the health problems that I had been through. When the woman from Fantasy came through the line taking the papers and reading them, she seemed moved by what Mom wrote. The Fantasy woman gave me a kiss on the head.

I thought that I had a chance with Fantasy giving me a computer. Probably not that day; after all it would take some time for them to get the hardware for me. Surely within the coming weeks, they'd invite me back to the TV studio for a heartfelt on-camera meeting with my new computer. But that was just a fantasy.

My parents weren't giving me a computer. NBC wasn't coughing up a computer. I had take matters into my own hands. The raffle.

I don't remember if it was premeditated or not. If I did plan it, I couldn't have planned it better. Either way, what I did took more cojones than my scrawny physique usually exhibited, but mostly a heap of luck.

Before we go on, I need to apologize to the parishioners of St. Jude's Church; and my mom; and the late Monsignor O'Connell; and to the rightful winner of the computer, who maybe would have had used the TI as a stepping stone to an amazing life in computer science. Sorry. I won't do it again.

Here's how it went down.

It was the end of the carnival day. Everyone was tired and ready to go home, and it was time for the raffle. Up on the dais was the master of ceremonies and the big spinning bin brimming with tickets. In front of the dais, hundreds and hundreds of people were watching and waiting for the drawing. And behind it were a few in-the-know kids who wanted a moment of glory on the stage, getting called up to draw the winning ticket for one of the six prizes. Adults always want a kid to pick the winning tickets. Because they're honest?

(The rewards could be more than just that moment of glory. One year, I drew the ticket for the grand prize, the Hawaii trip. The winner gave me $50 as a thank-you.)

But this year, I didn't ask to get called up to pull the ticket for the trip to Hawaii, or the $500 cash. When it was time to raffle off the computer, I volunteered for duty. I was called up, climbed onto the dais, and saw the huge crowd watching me. The bin was spinning.

My plan was simply to find my mom's ticket on top of the bin, and grab it as I sunk my hand into the massive pile of tickets.

The bin stopped spinning. I looked into it and saw thousands of tickets, but not the one I needed. They expected me to draw a ticket, so I said to the M.C., "Spin it again!" … and for some reason, he did.

Round and round it goes … and when it stopped, there, right on top, was my mom's ticket. The man opened the little hatch on the bin, and as I plunged my hand into the bin I grabbed the ticket between my thumb and index finger. At that second, I looked upward and closed my eyes and made a show of fishing around to the bottom of the barrel. When my hand emerged from the pile, Mom's ticket remained in my grasp. I handed it to the man, who read the name.

The ruse was a complete success. In my memory, the crowd clapped politely — but Mom remembers that a few people booed. The M.C. guy didn't say anything out of the ordinary. I don't think he knew who I was; that I was related to the winner, who worked at the church. And if he did, was he going to call me a cheater in front of that crowd of tired and hopeful Catholics? Would he risk alienating a trusted church employee?

I don't remember Mom ever saying a word to me about it. I'm sure I earned an incredulous look, but for some reason she decided not to ask me if I cheated, or how, or (horrors) just donate the computer back to the church. We just brought the box home, and it became mine.

If she was going to have a grifter for a son, I'm sure Mom would have preferred that I picked the ticket for the trip to Hawaii.

I used that computer every day after school for months. But I never loved the TI like the Atari 800 or even appreciated it as much as the TRS-80s at school. Maybe the guilt of the underhanded way that I had acquired it kept me from truly appreciating it? No, that wasn't it at all. Compared to the others I'd used, the TI just didn't seem like a great computer to me. (It still doesn't. I don't have one in my collection of computers today.)

First of all, the BASIC was terribly slow. Now, BASICs of the era were interpreted languages, which are always slower than compiled languages. The tradeoff is that they're much easier to program than a compiled language like assembly. But the TI BASIC was exceptionally slow; frustratingly slow. Decades later, I would learn why. Quoting Wikipedia: "TI BASIC was a double interpreted language, as the BASIC interpreter was itself written in a mid-layer interpreted byte-code language known as Graphics Programming Language, which was unique to the TI Home Computer." So it was an interpreted language running within another interpreted language, providing extra layers of sluggishness.

The wiki also says, "TI Extended BASIC improved execution speed somewhat by providing some functionality in assembly language." Now they tell me. I should have just learned assembly.

Another speed frustration for me was the cassette interface I had to use to save and load programs. Disk drives were fast and expensive; cassette tapes were slow and cheap. Although the TI could work with a disk drive, my ill-gotten computer didn't include one, so I paid a few dollars for the special cable that would let me connect it to my cassette recorder. Saving and loading my programs was slow, slow, slow.

So I programmed what I could, and I typed in programs from Compute! magazine, and I read the manuals and learned everything I could from the machine. Someone got me a typing tutorial cartridge, which helped me to increase my keyboarding speed — but did nothing for my technique. My hands flailed across the keyboard in ways that would make a typing teacher cringe.

That TI was only the first of two stolen computers that I would own.

HANDHELD GAMES

My daughter's Nintendo DS can play hundreds of games. A single cartridge in that handheld device can contain literally dozens of different games. My generation was the first to enjoy electronic handheld games, but back in the day each game played one game.

Perhaps the classic, first-to-jump-to-mind, early handheld game is Mattel Football. I had one, or maybe a friend had one that I borrowed, because I played it a lot. Players were represented by little red LEDs, which you'd try to move down the field by kicking or passing the little red LED ball. There's no way I would willingly play football, and I couldn't stand watching it (or any sport) on TV. Joe was constantly watching football on the living room TV; it was hard to get away from. I tried a few times to watch with him, I think in part so that we'd have something, anything, in common to talk about, but football was boring and stupid and dumb. However, replace hulking players with little red lights — apparently that was all I needed to enjoy football.

Other things that I did in handheld games that I might not have enjoyed in real life include escaping mazes. "Escape! 1000 Mazes" was a first-person shooter without the shooting. It was a first-person walker. You would see the perspective of a person inside a maze, and try to navigate your way out. The Interwebs say that it's fairly rare today — only 50,000 were produced. I don't know what happened to my maze game, but I guess I should have kept it for its rarity value.

I do still have my original Bandai Air Traffic Control game from 1981, and I know exactly why I still own it: I didn't like it that much, so it lived at my dad's house. He loved the game and played it all the time. I thought it was too hard. I did like the big screen and keypad full of complicated, colorful buttons — but I killed thousands and thousands of little red LED people as I sent their little red LED airplanes into the drink. (There are cool pictures of the game at www.handheldmuseum.com/Bandai/AirTraffic .htm — as well as information and pictures about many more of those '80s portable electronic games.)

Another handheld game that I had was Coleco's Zodiac: "The Astrology Computer." I don't know what Coleco was thinking in making this weird toy, nor what my parents were thinking when they got it for me. This little round calculator had the signs of the zodiac embossed on the outside edge.

Christmas morning, opening Air Traffic Controller. Also notice the Intellivision box in the background.

After you used the keypad to enter your birthday and a code for your place of birth, the machine would beep and boop for a while before displaying a series of numbers. You had to write down the numbers, then refer to the thick manual to find out what each of the codes meant about your horoscope. The game was useless without the manual to interpret the codes. I wonder why people didn't just read the newspaper for their horoscope. Most of all, I wonder why no one told me that astrology is crazy, made-up B.S. and that I shouldn't have wasted precious time or brain cells on it. Oh wait, I just remembered that my mom also had a handheld biorhythm calculator. Maybe they didn't know.

Quiz Wiz, also by Coleco, was another electronic game that was useless without the book, but at least it was vaguely educational. You would read a question in the book, along with four possible answers. Then you'd tap the question number and the answer (A, B, C, or D) on the keypad, which would light a light and beep to tell you if you were right or wrong. I had some general interest trivia books for it. Apparently there were 30 or so question books available, with titles like "The Ocean — Mankind's Last Frontier" and "Monsters, Vampires, Witches and Ghosts." Quiz Wiz was not fun. I saw one recently at a retro gaming convention and didn't have a hint of nostalgia for it. It was *that* not fun.

Perhaps the only handheld game that was both educational and actually fun was Texas Instruments' Speak & Spell. My cousin Todd and several of my other friends had it, and I think it actually taught me some spelling. It was amazing to hear a machine talk, and fun to try to make it say weird things. TI also made toys called Speak & Read and Speak & Math. They were not as fun. Sorry, TI.

The first handheld game that really played multiple games was Microvision, which was released in 1979 but defunct by 1981. By switching cartridges, it could play games like Breakout and pinball on a tiny, monochrome screen. I guess I sort of wanted one, but I wanted a lot of stuff and grew to be a happy and functional adult without it. One day, Joe promised that he'd buy me one, but in the same sentence he promised me a private stairway to my second-story bedroom and a lot of other weird things. He had just been in the hospital, and was out of his mind on pain meds. Even though I was eight or nine at the time, I knew that the Microvision — and the private stairway — were pipe dreams.

One of my all-time favorite toys wasn't a game at all. The Radio Shack 150-in-1 Electronic Project Kit consisted of a collection of capacitors, resistors, LEDs, switches, and other electronic components on a breadboard. It also came with wires and a thick book showing you how to wire the projects together. I built the telegraph, the high-gain audio amplifier, the project that made bird sounds, and probably 147 other projects. It was a truly educational toy.

Me and my 150-in-1 Electronic Project Kit.

Big Trak wasn't a handheld game, but was a great electronic toy. Big Trak was a programmable vehicle: you could use the keypad to tell it how to move — go forward, turn, backward — programming up to 16 steps in advance, then pressing GO and watching it follow your instructions.

It could shoot at stuff with a light on the front and laser noise. It had a "transport" add-on that could carry something around, then dump it out like a dump truck. (A TV commercial showed the Big Trak taking a circuitous route to deliver an apple to a hungry dad.) I had endless hours of fun creating obstacle courses, then programming the Big Trak to move around it.

I wasn't the only one with fond memories of that toy, because in 2010 a company released a modern version, Big Trak Jr. The toy looks and works the same but is smaller than the 1979 version. It's still fun, and now I get to play with it with my daughters. I love that geeks have managed to re-create and preserve the essence of that toy. There's a modern version of the Mattel Football game, too. The world is still waiting for updates of Quiz Wiz and Zodiac, The Astrology Computer.

CHAPTER 5
APPLE //C

By 1984, when I was in eighth grade, the TI wasn't cutting it anymore. The BASIC was slow and the tape drive was slow, and I felt like I had extracted all the interesting knowledge that I could from that machine. I was ready for a real computer. I still wanted an Atari, like the 800XL — the newest machine in the Atari line — but Mom and Joe thought the Ataris were toys, not serious computers for schoolwork.

The first Macintosh was released that year — it was a beautiful thing, but was ludicrously expensive. Then the October 1984 issue of Creative Computing arrived in my mailbox, and I fell in love with the sexy thing on the cover: the Apple //c. I asked for one for Christmas, and, to my surprise, got one.

It wasn't wrapped under the tree. The various boxes were so large that Santa left them off to the side of the tree with a blanket thrown over as the wrapping. Mom and Joe went all out, with the computer and a monochrome monitor, an Imagewriter printer, Print Shop and Flight Simulator II software. Of course I was thrilled.

That Christmas morning, Mom took a picture of me hugging the Apple //c boxes. I have re-created that picture with many of the Apple computers that I have owned since. I get older and the boxes get smaller, but the joy of a new computer to explore remains the same.

The //c was a deep and rich new realm to delve into. I subscribed to InCider, an Apple magazine; and bought books

Creative Computing's first look at the Apple //c sold me on it.

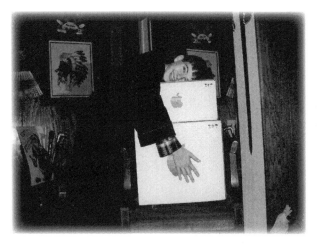

Giving the Apple //c a hug.

about programming in Applesoft BASIC. I flew around and around (but never learned to land) in Flight Simulator. I created art with Dazzle Draw and animation with Fantavision — an amazing program that let you draw two disparate frames, and it would create the animation to tie them together. I razed forests for my dabbling with Print Shop.

(Months later, I created a font for Print Shop — a character set that looked like an LCD calculator — and submitted it to Brøderbund. I didn't hear back for months, and eventually assumed they weren't going to respond. After I'd given up hope, I did receive a nice letter from the company, apologizing for taking so long to reply. It said my envelope had been lost in the office, and that they liked my font — but they had no plans to release any more add-on packs for Print Shop, so they couldn't use it. I was happy that they'd even consider it.)

The //c was sleek and sexy, bordering on portable, with its built-in disk drive and carrying handle. It was speedy (especially compared to the TI it replaced) and could display 80 columns of text with nice, clear letters. It had a whopping 128KB of memory, more than any computer I had used. The graphics weren't as good as Dad's Atari, and its sound capabilities were terrible, but the //c was a capable, fun computer that I was thrilled to use.

I wrote countless school papers and assignments using Bank Street Writer. The first time I sat down at the computer to write a paper, Mom yelled at me — why was I using the computer when I had homework to do? I explained that I was writing my paper. She said that I shouldn't be typing it until I had completely written it out by hand. It took some explaining to show her how I could write, and change the words, in a word processor — it wasn't necessary to have it perfect before you put fingers to keyboard, like with a typewriter.

A man named Deeroy lived a short walk from our house. Deeroy was an adult with a serious computer hobby.

The Apple //c in my room.

He owned a Commodore 64 and an Apple ///. It was probably the first computer that I used that had a hard drive. He treated that computer like a precious baby. Actually, he had a kid. He may have treated the computer more preciously than the kid. Deeroy was willing to let me use his software and borrow it, but he adamantly refused to let me copy it. Software piracy was still a matter of fact for me — I didn't have a lot of Apple software trading partners like I did for Dad's Atari. But Deeroy wasn't going to be one of them. He bought his software and expected others to do the same.

Deeroy introduced me to Wizardry (I know it's a classic, but I didn't find it interesting) and Little Computer People, which was a fun simulation of a guy who lived inside your computer. It was a lot like the Sims, if the memory in the computer could only handle one lonely little Sim.

I did a lot of programming on the //c. I dabbled in Logo, learning to draw pretty polygons on the screen; but spent most of my time with Applesoft BASIC. I wrote a program to quiz me on vocabulary words for Spanish class, and a program that printed random insults. I wrote a program that let you change the error messages in BASIC, and submitted it to a computer magazine. I didn't get a reply, but the program wasn't really anything new — that trick had been done before, and better, by other programmers.

I wrote a huge amount of — but didn't finish — a text adventure game in which it was your job to set up the rides at a carnival. Before I abandoned the project, I could walk all around the fairgrounds by typing compass directions: I had the mapping and navigation complete. I think the complexity of the language parser was probably the stumbling block that kept me from completing the game.

TEXT ADVENTURES

My attempt at writing a text adventure on the Apple wasn't successful, but I did spend a lot of time playing text adventure games, and completed several. Having the //c at home was the first time I had enough time in front of a computer to really dive into interactive fiction. (There were adventure games for the TI, but I didn't know about them; and a few minutes at lunchtime wasn't enough for me to get too far in adventures at school.) I played Colossal Cave Adventure, Mystery House, Zork, Hitchhiker's Guide to the Galaxy, Suspended (which seemed crazy hard; maybe I should try that one again), and many others.

If you've never played a text adventure game, here's what it looks like. The stuff I type follows the > symbol:

```
You are behind the white house. In one corner
of the house
there is a window which is slightly ajar.

> open window

With great effort, you open the window far
enough to allow passage.

> enter

You are in the kitchen of the white house. A
table seems to have
```

```
been used recently for the preparation of food.
A passage leads to
the west, and a dark staircase can be seen
leading upward. To the
east is a small window which is open.

On the table is an elongated brown sack,
smelling of hot peppers.
A clear glass bottle is here.
The glass bottle contains: A quantity of water.

> take all

brown sack:
Taken.
glass bottle:
Taken.

>
```

I really enjoyed those text adventure games, particularly the ones from Infocom, a game publisher that specialized in them. I loved to read — the best adventure games had great writing that I could really get into, plus puzzles that would challenge my brain for days. I loved trying to solve those puzzles — like how to get the babel fish in my ear in Hitchhiker's Guide. I did not love navigating mazes. Too many games had mazes. I also loved the flash of insight that could come during lunch or as I was falling asleep — when potential answers to puzzles would pop into my head while I wasn't consciously thinking about the puzzle at all. It's the same magical part of the brain that provided answers to programming problems, and today gives me ideas for my business.

When I couldn't figure out the answers to the puzzles for myself, the only place to turn to was InvisiClues. Before the days of loading up walkthroughs online, you had to get a hint book. Infocom had a unique way of gently delivering clues: hints were printed in invisible ink, revealed when you used the special pen. Not every bookstore had the InvisiClues books, and more than once Mom patiently drove me to bookstores hither and yon so I could buy them.

The folks at Infocom also published a quarterly newsletter which I loved to read — it was always exciting to get it in the mail. At first the newsletter was called The New Zork Times, until a certain New York newspaper threatened to sue them ... so Infocom renamed it to The Status Line. It was basically a marketing tool to tell their audience about new games, but there were also a lot of silly articles and cartoons, letters from players, and interviews. (Thanks to the Interwebs, you can read all those newsletters here: infodoc.plover.net/nzt/)

In the spring 1986 issue, Infocom announced a "Design a Better Envelope Contest," asking readers to submit art that would be included on the outside of the mailing envelope of a future edition. They would pick one winner, who would get an Infocom game of his or her choice. I could barely draw a stickman, but stepdad Joe was a phenomenal professional artist. I asked him to draw a cartoon for my entry to the contest, and he agreed. I described what I wanted: Arthur Dent from The Hitchhiker's Guide to the Galaxy, surrounded by some of the stuff from the game: a towel, a spaceship, a toothbrush, tea, a flowerpot, and so on. He had never read the books or played the game, but he whipped up a cartoon in no time. It looked professional — down to the halftone pattern that he used for Arthur's dressing gown. He signed my initials to it, and I submitted it to the contest.

There was supposed to be one winner of the envelope contest, but they must have gotten a lot of good entries. The summer 1986 issue of The Status Line read:

"The competition was stiff. Literally HUNDREDS of budding Picassos submitted their finest Louvre-quality works. ... The judges of the contest, while highly discriminating, are also terribly soft-hearted. With hearts the consistency of oatmeal, they couldn't bear to limit the contest to just one winner. They instead wanted to declare everybody a winner, but we had to hold them to six. So, the SIX first place winners are: Chris Douglas of Austin, TX; Jeff Nelsen of Torrance, CA; Kevin Savetz of Agoura Hills, CA" [... and blah blah blah some other people.]

My — I mean, Joe's — art was finally printed on the envelope for the winter 1987 issue of the newsletter. That must have been an agonizing wait — from summer of 1986 to winter 1987 — to see the cartoon actually show up in the mail, with a return address from Infocom. I don't actually remember the wait, but I wasn't exactly a paragon of patience: it must have been torture. When it finally did appear for the world to see, it was uncredited! No one would know that I drew that fabulous cartoon that I didn't really draw.

The newsletter ran a correction in the next issue:

P.O. Box 478
Cresskill, New Jersey 07626

Address Correction Requested

Arthur Dent appears to be on the verge of panic in the winning cartoon.

"It was bound to happen ... Believe it or not, something went awry at The Status Line. We never thought we'd need a corrections blurb, but here it is. First, our sincere apologies to Kevin Savetz of Agoura Hills, CA. Kevin's award-winning drawing from The Hitchhiker's Guide to the Galaxy graced the envelope of the last issue, but we did not credit him in the issue. Please send lots of money to Kevin in care of TSL."

No one sent me lots of money, of course, but back in the summer of 1986 when they announced the winners, Infocom did send me a game of my choice. I chose A Mind Forever Voyaging, a brand new game in which you play the part of a sentient computer. I *had* to finish it. Having won it in the contest, I was invested in that game. Luckily, it wasn't one of their difficult games — it was more about exploration of a place over time.

That is my tale of fleeting fame in the Infocom newsletter. I had an idea for another cartoon, a spoof of Infocom game titles. For instance, A Mind Forever Voyaging would become A Mind Forever Wandering, with a cartoon of a kid in class but not paying attention. I don't think I asked Joe to draw it, and that's probably just as well. The spring 1989 issue of The Status Line was the final one — the cartoon probably never would have been printed.

Somewhere between then and now, the term changed from "text adventure games" to "interactive fiction." Which makes sense, because they're not all adventures, and they're not all games. (Then again, I don't think they're all fiction either.) Today there's a small but thriving community of interactive fiction players and authors. There are several annual contests where programmers compete to create the best interactive fiction. You can play oldies like Zork and fantastic newer stuff like Lost Pig on just about any platform, including your phone. If you're interested, check out www.ifwiki.org and www.ifcomp.org and www.sparkynet .com/spag/ to get started.

THE MAILBOX

The Infocom newsletter was hardly the only nerdy thing that came in the mail for me. The mailbox was a primary connection, an artery, to information about computers. Before I had a modem of my own, if I wanted information about technology — and I wanted information about technology — it came either from the library or in the mail.

Computer magazines were my favorite source of knowledge. I subscribed to Compute! (the exclamation mark was a part of the title) and Creative Computing, both of which covered multiple computer platforms. Dad subscribed to Antic, which was all about Atari. My friend Marc had a subscription to A.N.A.L.O.G., the other big Atari magazine, and let me borrow his issues after he read them. (A.N.A.L.O.G. stood for Atari News And Lots Of Games, not to be confused with the sci-fi magazine Analog.) I subscribed to other computer magazines on and off through the years too.

When I was out shopping with Mom at a bookstore, the mall, or the market, I would do my best to acquire whatever other magazines they had, like Family Computing or Popular Computing. Mom remembers those trips too: "When I went to the market you were my coupon man. You ran around the store and picked up the items we had coupons for. It was in the times it was OK to have a child go off by themselves in the store. You always ended up with a computer magazine under your arm mixed in with the coupon purchases. The magazine cost more than what the coupons were valued at, but it was fun and I hoped I was showing you some sort of shopping skills and money-saving ideas — or perhaps it was how to scheme Mom for a $5 magazine."

I read them all from cover to cover, including the articles about computer systems that I didn't own, the advertisements, the letters, and the tiny classified ads in the back. Even if an article didn't particularly interest me, I wanted to know everything that I could.

Computer magazines were more interesting then than they are now. Back then, using computers was primarily a hobby for most of the readership: the articles and letters were often about exploring the systems, expanding the limits of what was possible with the hardware, and experimenting. Most of today's computer magazines, on the other hand, are primarily about using machines as the tools they have become, they're usually focused more on how to get work done than appealing to the creative interests of curious hobbyists. Computer Power User might be an exception, as it has regular sections about modding hardware and tweaking software.

Some magazines had a feature which is unnecessary now: type-in programs. Readers would submit programs (or magazine staff would write them), the magazine would print them, then readers would spend long hours typing them in. Many of the programs were games, but there were also useful utility programs, even full-fledged applications. Compute!, for instance, published SpeedScript, a full-fledged word processor in assembly language. But the majority of the programs were in BASIC, because the majority of home computers had BASIC built in. If a magazine covered multiple systems, like Compute! did, they would sometimes print four or five or six versions of the same program, each tuned to the various BASIC dialects.

This point cannot be stressed though: typing in the programs was drudgery. You'd read a part of a line of code from the magazine, then turn to the screen and type it, back to the magazine to read, back to the screen to tap it in. Some programs were harder to key in than others. If you didn't type the code in perfectly, the program wouldn't work right (or at all). Sometimes Dad and I would work together: I'd read the code aloud and he would type it into the Atari.

It was drudgery, but if you paid attention you could learn a ton about programming.

Here's a sample of Microids, a program that Dad and I typed in from the May 1983 issue of Antic magazine — and had a lot of fun playing together:

```
1000 FOR L=1 TO 150:SHD=INT(15*RND(1))
1010 C=INT(5*RND(1)):HUE=INT(16*RND(1)):SETCO
     LOR C,U,SHD:SOUND 2,(C+HUE)*10,12,8:SOUND
     1,(C+HUE)*3,0,8:NEXT L
1020 SOUND 0,0,0,0:SOUND 1,0,0,0:SOUND
     2,0,0,0:RD=RD+1:ADMIC=1
1030 SCR=SCR+PTS:GOTO 500
5000 GRAPHICS 18:SETCOLOR 0,0,0:POSITION 6,2:?
     #6;"MICROIDS"
5020 FOR L=1 TO 70:POKE 712,INT(16*RND(0))*16+INT(1
     6*RND(0)):
     SOUND 0,PEEK(53770),12,8:NEXT L:SOUND 0,0,0,0
```

```
5030 GRAPHICS 18:IF STRIG(0)=0 THEN 5030
5040 SETCOLOR 4,7,2:POSITION 3,2:? #6;" fire
     joystick"
     POSITION 7,4:? #6;" button":POSITION 1,6
```

It goes on like that for 80 lines.

Indecently, the magazine's description of the Microids game starts like this: "It is the year 1993. Scientists have developed a new type of germ warfare called Microids. This deadly combination of genetic engineering and submicroscopic electronics has produced an almost indestructible man-made microbe ..." It's sad and funny and makes me feel old when the future is 20 years ago. Also weird: the game was written by a Baptist clergyman.

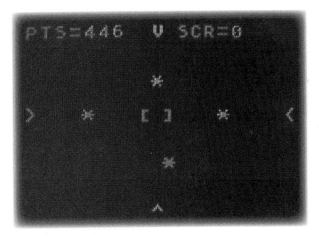

Screenshot of Microids.

Here's some of the code from Chopperoids, a particularly nasty-to-type game in machine language, from the December 1983 issue of Compute! magazine:

```
3608:169.014,133,011,024,096,215
3614:000,020,000,014,008,014,086
3620:024,096,169,060,141,002,016
```

You can see how typing a few hundred lines of that could bring on headaches. (Though I typed those three lines by hand just for old times' sake.)

Even if you typed the program in perfectly, sometimes — maddeningly often — you'd discover that the magazine hadn't printed it perfectly. They left a part out, or printed a buggy version, for instance. So you'd have to save your work and wait a month or two for them to print a correction, and hope that would take care of the problem. (Compute! magazine was notorious for this, so much so that we started calling it Kaput! When you ran the programs, they would just go kaput.) In the meantime, you've invested hours typing in the program and can't help but feel that the problem must be on your end, so you spend more time poring over the code that you typed, comparing it to the code in the magazine. Chopperoids was one of those programs.

Then, after you and everyone else got the program working, sometimes the magazine's letters section would print improvements submitted by other readers — change this line of code to make the game easier, or faster, or better. Add a few lines of code to add a useful new feature. It was a slow sort of collaborative programming project.

(On my trip to Europe with Dad after sixth grade, I discovered that England had an entirely different set of computer magazines. Dad and I bought one and, when we got home, typed in its BASIC game, "Neutralize," which had something to do with cleaning up toxic spills.)

When modems became popular, you could just dial into a BBS or CompuServe and download the magazine programs, ready to run because someone else had typed them in — or they came directly from the magazine itself. Heck, you didn't even need the magazine: you could enjoy the games and utilities, as long as you could get along without printed instructions.

I'd also fill out and mail in the "reader service cards" in magazines — the little postcards in the back that made it easy to request more information from the advertisers. I'd get all sorts of brochures and catalogs in the mail. Online services were particularly interesting to me: I read and re-read the brochures from The Source and BRS/After Dark, and gadget catalogs from companies such as DAK and Radio Shack. I was particularly excited to receive the occasional cassette tape in the mail, like one with sample audio from the Yamaha Clavinova digital keyboard, and one demonstrating Covox Voice Master, a speech synthesis product. It was multimedia junk mail.

I didn't know him back then, but my friend Jason Scott was more methodical in the reader service card information quest. Quoting him:

> Now, to a reasonable person, say, an adult reading the magazine, they might fill out one or two circles to get a catalog without having to call somewhere or waste postage. But that wasn't the case to me at 12 years old.

This was an opportunity to get all these wonderful companies to send me neat stuff for free. So I did what anyone in my position (and perspective) would do.

… I circled them all.

Dozens of letters would arrive every day; my mother had no idea what to make of it. I started using multiple names, just so I could roughly track what flyers, leaflets and catalogs were coming as a result of which magazine. I quickly figured out that Creative Computing had the most active companies sending me stuff, so I'd hit them up for even more. My room started collecting piles of ads, papers, what-have-you being mailed to me. …

Years later, I finally took the box out of storage in my basement, sorted through it, moved things around, stacked by size, and began the process of cataloging and understanding exactly what I had. And the short answer is, I have a ton of fascinating stuff! Catalogs of companies now long gone (and forgotten), brochures promising you the world in eight bits, newsletters of what amazing things were around the corner.

A kid wanting information about his hobby is understandable. The part where Jason had vision (or maybe it was just fortuitous laziness) is where he kept all of it, grew up, scanned it, and put all of it online as part of archive.org's collection. He calls it the Reader Service Collection. You can browse it here: www.archive.org/details/readerservice

and read his blog post about it, which I quoted above, here: ascii.textfiles.com/archives/3136.

For me, besides the catalogs, pamphlets, brochures, and cassette tapes, the bonus was the pieces of mail that contained floppy disks with demo software, which I would format and re-use to store my own programs. A couple of software companies, such as Andrew Tobias' Managing Your Money, could be counted on for a free demo disk almost every time I asked, every month or so. The rarest, most prized floppies came from the handful of companies that sent picture disks: where the floppy sleeve had an image or an interesting graphic on it instead of being a single color, like most disks. Buick sent a pair of nifty picture disks with full-color pictures of cars on the sleeves. I still have those, so I guess I have a little bit of Jason's vision, too.

BOOKS

Books were another fantastic source of information about computers. My schools' libraries had a small selection of computer books, and I went to local libraries too. The Agoura library didn't have a great selection of computer books as I recall, but they did have an Apple // that patrons could use, and a selection of software that you could check out to use on the library computer. After I got an Apple //c, I spent some time at the library, huddled close to the Apple's screen so the librarians wouldn't see that I was methodically copying their software. The Thousand Oaks library, which Mom would drive me to occasionally but became far more accessible once I had a driver's license, had a wider range of computer books.

The books that stand out in my mind, the ones that I spent hours and hours poring over, were BASIC Computer Games and More BASIC Computer Games by David Ahl. David was the editor of Creative Computing magazine, and the books were just as interesting as the magazine. More BASIC Computer Games (which I owned first) contained "84 challenging new games to play on your personal computer, all in BASIC and complete with program listing and sample run." So, like those program listings in computer magazines, here we had more programs to type in carefully.

The games were written in Microsoft BASIC, so they would work on the many computer systems that used that flavor of BASIC. (Frustratingly, the BASICs on the Atari and Apple computers had enough quirky differences that I'd sometimes need to change a lot of the code to make the programs work.) I actually didn't spend as much time typing those programs as I did reading the BASIC code and figuring out how they worked. Or I would just read and re-read the sample runs — where the book would just show each game in progress.

If the games had graphics at all, they were simple ASCII maps or graphs. Imagine a game called Motorcycle Jump — there's a lot of potential there, right? Take all of that potential fun and remove any ideas you might have had about graphics or sound. Here's part of the sample run:

```
HOW MANY BUSSES WILL YOU TRY TO JUMP? 5
   5 BUSSES! THAT'S 75 FEET!
WHAT RAMP ANGLE WILL YOU USE? 22
HOW FAST WILL YOU LEAVE THE RAMP? 46
   GOOD LUCK!
THERE HE GOES!!!!
*********HE'S SHORT OF THE RAMP .....
I THINK HE'S HURT......
WELL, KILLER, THE DOCTOR SAYS YOU BROKE YOUR:
R.ARM
PRIDE
L.ARM
BACK
BUTT
```

The book also includes versions of games that became true classics, like ELIZA and Hunt The Wumpus. And, I'm noticing now, more than its fair share of compute-the-trajectory games. I already mentioned Motorcycle Jump. Here's another, called Schmoo.

```
MUD SLINGER ELEVATION? 39
DIRECTIONAL ANGLE OF MUD SLINGER? 34
YOU MISSED THE SCHMOO AT ( 29007, 9760 ).
YOUR MUD HIT ( 27707 , 25433 ).
```

and another game, called Artillery 3:

```
PLAYER 1 SHOOTING AT? 2
FIRING ANGLE? 70
   YOU OVERSHOT BY 808.207 FEET.
```

I guess when the book was published in 1979, estimating angles to shoot things was very exciting. Some of the other games are downright odd. For instance: "Father" simulates a debate with your father about going out on Saturday night. After you win or lose the debate, Saturday night approaches and you must decide whether or not to actually go out. Another weird one is "Nomad": Gramma Nomad is a person who doesn't really know where she wants to live, so she moves to a new house every game. Then she sends you a telegram asking you to visit her. The object of the game is to successfully navigate your way through the streets of Garbanzo City to her house.

Besides the games themselves, the other interesting thing about the BASIC Computer Games books was the great cartoons by an artist named George Beker. He drew cartoons of robots doing various odd things (playing poker, watching TV, playing with toy trains …) Those "Beker bot" cartoons were interspersed throughout the the books.

You can read the book in its entirety, and see the cartoons, at my Web site: www.atariarchives.org/more basicgames/. I'll say more about creating that site later in this book, but I'm going to jump ahead and talk about it a little right now.

I had gotten permission from David Ahl to put More BASIC Computer Games and a slew of his other books online. I found David through America Online, back before he (or most anyone else) had a Web site. We struck up a friendship, and I was (and remain) impressed by his willingness to openly share the material from Creative

Computing books and magazines. A few years later, he decided to clean out his basement, and sold me a bunch of old books and magazines, which is why today I have French and German editions of the BASIC Computer Games books.

I put the BASIC Computer Games books online with loving care, complete with metadata and foreign language cover variations. They were online for years, until 2010 when I got an e-mail from George Beker, the bot cartoonist. He was working on his own site about the bot art and didn't want the images on my Web site competing for attention on the Interwebs, at least not without a watermark or otherwise obscured. This was worrying: if he demanded that I remove his art from my online versions of the books — certainly within his rights — they wouldn't be as interesting, and the fans of the books reminiscing with my Web site would certainly be disappointed.

After some back-and-forth e-mail, I found out that Beker is a super-nice and interesting guy. We worked out a complicated deal that we were both happy with: I would permit watermarks on the bot drawings at atariarchives .org, but he would do the work of adding them. I would add a link to a new version of the BASIC Computer Games book — a fan had ported the games to a modern language called Small Basic — as well as to Beker's own site (which is at www.BekerBots.com and is worth visiting. He sells a PDF called "Bot Folio" that includes all of the bots he ever drew, along with his commentary about them.) The best part of the deal for me: in exchange for a donation to

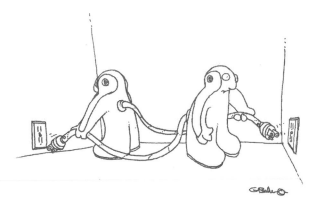

This is one of
my favorite
Beker bot
cartoons.

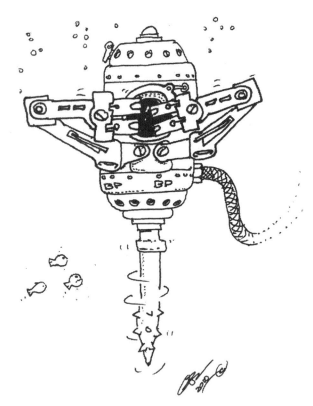

Beker's BP
bot, the
original of
which graces
my office.

his wife's nonprofit organization, Beker would give me a original bot drawing.

After all was said and done, everyone was happy and I have an original Beker bot framed on my office wall. The drawing is of an ocean exploration bot. The letters "BP" (for British Petroleum) are visible on the bot's casing. (This all occurred shortly after BP spilled 4.9 million barrels of oil in the Gulf of Mexico.) I asked Beker if the bot is evil. He answered, "I agree BP-bot is 'evil' in its way, but stupid as well — a winning combination."

ASHTON-TATE

My dad had a friend, who I'll call Paul. Paul was this cool guy who happened to work at Ashton-Tate. If you've never heard of Ashton-Tate, I don't blame you. It was once one of the big three software publishers, along with Microsoft and Lotus, but then pfft … it became a footnote in history. The company was best known for dBASE, its database application.

Paul knew I was into computers, he had access to computer stuff at his work, and he shared the bounty. He gave a me a copy of dBASE III Developer Edition, an expensive PC program in an enormous (and heavy) box. I was all, "Thanks, but … what I am supposed to do with this?" Paul said, "Do whatever you want with it." So it sat around my room in its shrink-wrap for a while. I ended up selling it to a friend's parent for a couple hundred dollars, which was a huge windfall for me. Paul also gave me a shiny black jacket with the Ashton-Tate logo on the back, which I wore to school and everywhere else for months.

The best thing that Paul had to share was floppy disks — piles and piles of floppy disks. This was 1985 or so, and floppy disks were still expensive: $10 for a box of 10 disks wasn't an unreasonable price. With Dad's and my burgeoning collection of pirated Atari software, our appetite for blank floppies was great. Paul gave us stacks of floppy disks — disks that were (the majority of them, anyway) perfectly good but had failed the verification process while Ashton-Tate software was being copied to them. They didn't come with protective sleeves like they did when you bought a box of disks, so I often made disk covers out of printer paper.

One day, Dad and I were able to visit Paul in his office. I don't know if it was in Ashton-Tate's headquarters in Torrence (so says Wikipedia) or a satellite office. But it was impressive to me: the room of cubicles, the row of disk-duplicating machines, the enormous crate of "dead" floppy disks. It was my first time seeing where software got made, and it was awesome.

One evening while Dad and I were having dinner at Paul's apartment, Dad stepped out of the room and Paul took that opportunity to cop a feel. He did a fantastic job of making it seem like he was just goofing around, but I suddenly got it: why he was plying me with cool stuff.

I didn't tell anyone, but I made sure I wasn't alone with him again. I did let him keep giving us floppy disks. I mean, wow, free floppy disks, that was something special.

CHAPTER 6
HIGH SCHOOL

In 1985, Back To the Future and The Breakfast Club were on the silver screen. A.E. Wright Middle School handed me a diploma and a journalism award for my work on the school newspaper. I was on to high school. At Calabasas High School, my interests in computers and writing continued, plus photography was added to the mix.

If you aren't from Southern California, you may have heard about the city of Calabasas or its high school for one of two reasons. One: the Kardashians live there. Two: the rich, parent-murdering Menendez brothers. I went to Calabasas High with Erik Menendez.

Although middle school had been all TRS-80s, all the time, Calabasas High School had a mish-mash of computers, mostly IBM PC compatibles and Apple //s. In fact, I don't think there was a TRS-80 on campus. But there were plenty of other computers to explore and learn from.

The lab in the math building had a bunch of Apple //s and some basic PCs. The PC in the library was far more interesting: it had a CD-ROM-based encyclopedia (a whole encyclopedia in the palm of your hand!), InfoTrac databases, and dial-up access to other library catalogs.

Everything on that computer was locked down with passwords and menus to prevent students from doing anything other than proscribed research. But the computer was in a small room, relatively private compared to the main library area, which afforded me the opportunity to figure out ways to hack into the machine. The first goal was simply to get to the DOS prompt and explore the data on the hard drive. Once I accomplished that, the next goal was to use the modem to dial numbers other than the library database. I used that machine to call into Weird City, all the way in the 213 area code, on the school's dime.

The school's resident geek was the science teacher, Mr. Pollock. The librarian wasn't terribly tech-savvy, so it fell to Mr. Pollock (who was such a geek he had a ham radio in his classroom) to lock down the library computer against kids like me. He would discover that someone had hacked the library machine and install a counter-measure. I'd find a new work-around. We played cat and mouse like that over the course of weeks.

Eventually, Mr. Pollock called me to his classroom. I wasn't in any of his classes. I must have been caught — I couldn't think of any other reason that he would want to talk to me. I was scared — terrified about the penalty that was about to befall me. But Mr. Pollock did something that

I didn't expect: he told me that he couldn't beat me at the security game, and asked for my help. In exchange for helping him keep other students from fussing with the library computer, we had the tacit understanding that I could do whatever I wanted with it.

Although I never did have a class with him, Mr. Pollock and I became friends and have kept in contact via e-mail over the years. When I showed him a draft of this chapter, he shared a story of his own: "Prior to the Apple //e, teachers had to retype classroom handouts every time the masters wore out. I bought an interface, Qpid, to connect the //e to my Silver Reed typewriter. I'd wow the other staff members when the computer/typewriter combination typed several copies of a handout. Magical!"

I was terrible at math. What kind of nerd is bad at math? A terrible nerd. I began to lose traction in seventh or eighth grade, and by high school my math grades were a wreck — Cs and Ds all around. Math class often left me weeping in frustration. My geometry teacher gave me a D-minus, which was a gift — I had earned an F. I was so interested in computers but so bad at math — my teachers and parents didn't understand that at all. I didn't understand why they didn't understand: I saw no connection between the logical — but flexible — rules of programming a computer and the exacting, inflexible rules of algebra. In my mind, computers had nothing to do with math. My brain was more suited to writing, photography, and programming: things that allowed for creativity, and didn't have absolute right or wrong answers.

THE NEWSPAPER

Most of my computer time at school wasn't hacking in the library; it was just typing. I was on the editorial staff of the school newspaper, the Calabasas Courier, which meant using an Apple //e to type in the handwritten articles that other students submitted. Using any high-tech gadget is a whole lot less fun when you're a data entry drone. I would type the text of each article (but not the headline) into a word processor, then format the margins to the width of the newspaper column. Next, I would print the articles on a dot-matrix printer and cut off the excess paper so it was just the width of the text column. Finally, I would apply glue to the back of the sheet and carefully lay it out on the newspaper template. You had to be exact: if the column wasn't positioned straight on the template, it would come out crooked on every copy of the finished paper. Headlines had to be created using a special machine that printed letters one at a time onto clear plastic strips, which also had to be glued to the page. It produced much better-looking headlines than a dot-matrix printer could generate.

That was pretty much the state of the art for small newspaper publishing everywhere, until the Macintosh and Pagemaker came along.

One semester, I was the editor of the entertainment section of the paper, so I wrote and read a lot of reviews of albums and movies. One article that I wrote was about "Personics," a machine that was going to be available in record stores everywhere. You could select songs from its list like a jukebox, then the Personics machine would create a custom cassette tape for you containing just those songs. It was a mix-tape machine. It was a pre-pre-pre-iTunes machine.

Enter your local record store, and you may be surprised by the massive machine dominating a portion of the store, attracting customers' attention. The machine is called "Personics." It has numeric key pads, and LCD panels, and digital headphones. The idea behind it is unique. ... Songs cost from 50 cents to $1.25 each. Eventually there will be more than 15,000 songs available to purchase. The machine is available to preview songs as well. To hear a song, just put on the attached headphones, enter the catalog number of the tune, and hear a short segment of the song. After the selection has been made, giving a completed order blank to a store employee completes the work. The tape will be ready in a few minutes.

I quoted a company representative who said, "Half of the [people] we interviewed said they wished it was around ten years before." It certainly wasn't around ten years after. I ended the article with: "Personics claims a technical patent is pending on the product, so competition in the future is unlikely." That's for sure. Personics was a technology before its time.

In addition to writing, every student on the newspaper staff was required to sell a certain amount of advertising in the paper each semester. I hated that part of the job. Joe had a friend named Dick who was a private investigator.

(Yes, a private eye named Dick.) One day, I asked Dick if he would place an ad in the school paper — to my surprise, he agreed right away. He bought a full page ad, meeting my advertising sales quota for the year ... and practically guaranteeing no new business for himself whatsoever. I mean, what high school kid is going to hire a private investigator? It was a kind thing to do to help me out — and I think it's a safe bet it was the only advertisement for a private eye in the Calabasas Courier ever.

THE DARKROOM

I studied photography for three-quarters of my high school career.

Some of my time in photography class was spent examining the work of Diane Arbus and Imogen Cunningham, but most of it was spent in the school's darkroom. The room was enormous, with two rows of enlargers flanking the walls and a long steel sink dominating the center. I would arrive early to mix the foul-smelling chemicals, always remembering to follow the mantra: "Do what you oughta — add the acid to the watah."

Chemicals mixed, the other students filed in, looking pale in the room's surprisingly bright yellow light. During some procedures, such as experiments with lithography, the yellow lights were switched off in favor of dim red bulbs. It would take my eyes several minutes to become accustomed to the light, but I didn't have to wait that long to get to work, the layout and contents of the room were so familiar.

The darkroom at my high school is gone, probably replaced with two rows of sleek iMacs loaded with Photoshop. Rather than learning how to increase grain by using hot water in the developer solution, I imagine today's students learn how to apply a filter to do so. Rather than waving a handcrafted piece of cardboard-on-a-wire under the enlarger's light to soften an area of a print, they learn about manipulating image layers in software.

Some of my most memorable hours of high school were spent in that darkroom, which I am sure sounds more than little pathetic. Sometimes as we worked on our projects, my fellow students and I would sing. One boy whose name I have since forgotten knew the words to countless James Taylor tunes. He would lead us in renditions of "Your Smiling Face" and "Carolina In My Mind" as we watched our images appear like magic in the plastic trays. Alone, I would sing Talking Heads or scat, with little regard for my inability to carry a tune, my volume, or the classrooms sharing the adjacent walls. When I walked into the bright light of the classroom to examine my print, Mrs. Phillips might shoot me a look, but that didn't matter. Morale in the darkroom was high, people were enjoying their time in her class, why would she squelch our joy?

In that darkroom, I fell in like with Amie, an older woman who already had a boyfriend called Drew. In that darkroom, I experimented with making poster-sized prints, bas relief black-and-white lithographs, and watched a stoner named James deftly craft a bong from aluminum foil. If the cops are coming, just ball it up, man.

Traditional darkroom photography is a dying art. If you were to rattle off a long list of reasons why digital photography is superior, I wouldn't argue with you — it is superior, for all the reasons you just listed. But today's photography students, hunched in front of their rows of computers, don't get to sing in harmony while manipulating their pictures. I don't imagine that applying the Burn-In Filter can effect the level of joy that I felt using my hands to shape the light that streamed onto photo paper. For that reason alone, paper-and-chemical photography will never really die. Not because some curmudgeon refuses to give up his Beseler enlarger and his Underwood typewriter, but because there is art in the process of creating art. In hand-burning an underexposed corner, in crooning sappy songs while you work, in gliding through the pale yellow light. There's no Photoshop filter for that.

CHAPTER 7
IBM PC XT

One day, I graduated from the Apple //c to an IBM PC XT. This was some serious computing power, with 640KB of memory (an impressive boost from 128KB in the Apple,) a CGA color monitor and hard drive. It was my first computer with a hard disk drive, which could hold a whopping ten megabytes of programs and data.

I don't remember exactly when this happened — perhaps 1987, the tail end of my sophomore year of high school. The computer wasn't a birthday or Christmas gift; it seems like the XT appeared on an otherwise ordinary day — except for the massive beige box which showed up on the dining room table one afternoon. I was thrilled. Stunned is probably a better word.

Joe brought the computer home from work. He said that his employer had upgraded the computers and was letting employees buy the older PCs. I learned months later that the story was only partially true: the only true part was that he brought the computer home from work. I'll never know the details or his reasoning, but apparently he just put one of the office computers in the trunk of his car, drove home, and gave it to me.

Some time later he was fired for other acts of thievery. I don't know if the company ever learned specifically about the missing computer. If they did, it was too late — by that time I had loaded the XT with XTree and Police Quest and StarFlight and Turbo Pascal and 9.8 megabytes of other goodness. That PC, which may have started its life designing missile defense systems, ended up getting me through part of high school and my entire college career.

This machine was a true blue IBM PC. Even then it was becoming clear to me that IBM-compatible computers were going to become the dominant computer platform. The days of a dozen flavors of mostly-incompatible computer brands were winding down. That was sad, because the differences in the technology and capabilities of various brands of computers — Commodores and Apple //s and Texas Instruments and so on — were a big part of what made them interesting. Also, the IBM was primarily a *business* machine. They were large and beige. The PC's graphics were inferior to some of the computers that had been available for years: it could only show four colors at a time in its low-resolution graphics mode, and just one color on a black background in the high-resolution mode. By comparison, the Apple // could show 16 colors in its high-res mode. The PC's sound capability was awful: it could make a beep sound from its tiny internal speaker, and that was about it. Dad's aging Atari could play music in four-part harmony, and yet the expensive, newer PC could go "beep."

This wasn't my first exposure to an IBM machine. Dad had by now had his fill of teaching high school, and was running a travel agency in the Fox Hills Mall. There was an IBM PC AT — the next step up in the line — there. Also, my neighbor Jeff, a couple of years older than I was, had an IBM PC of his own, in his room, which I played with occasionally. (Not too long after, Jeff was indicted for credit card fraud. I'm not implying there's a connection there at all.)

One thing that I loved about the IBM PC was the manuals. Thick, hefty three-ring binders packed with details about using the Disk Operating System (DOS), and programming in BASIC, and seemingly every technical aspect of the machine. They were imposing and impressive just lined up on the bookshelf, and a never-ending source of technical reading material.

I just went to Google to look for a picture of those binders, and discovered another blog entry from my friend Jason Scott, who did a fantastic job of describing IBM's manuals. (ascii.textfiles.com/archives/2269) Quoting him:

> *If it was intended to imbue a sense of power and confidence, to give the impression that IBM was here and everything was going to be OK, it did it in spades for me. … How could a kid not be impressed with something like this? How could anyone not be, especially if it was the first time they encountered a business-grade manual? After all, the IBM PC was going to*

be business-grade, and having a reference document nearby in such a perfect layout was fine. ...

There really was a pride about it, here. Of craftsmanship, of IBM throwing people at the problem and those people having a lot of meetings and deciding what kind of a manual would, before you even turned the machine on, make you feel like you'd made the right choice.

At 4.77 MhZ, the XT wasn't slow. It wasn't super fast, either, but it was pleasantly speedy. Despite the limited graphics and sound, it was fun to use. I loved to explore the DOS commands, automate things with batch files, and play a whole new set of games. Sitting down at the machine was a different experience than any computer I had used before: it was imposing and powerful. The keyboard was heavy, and emitted a serious clacking noise when you typed. (It's a keyboard feel that I miss, especially compared to the tiny, almost spongy keyboards that are common on Apple products now.) The computer itself was large and heavy, really a monster compared to the lithe little Apple //c that I had been using. Even the power switch was impressive, a big red toggle that made a distinct snap when you switched the computer on, which was was followed by that beep and a whirr as the hard drive went to work.

Once I had fully moved into the PC, I sold the Apple //c and all of the related books and software to a man who worked at the church with my mom.

On my 17th birthday, mid-1988, my Atari friend Tim brought me an NEC V20 chip, a replacement for the XT's

8088 CPU. He said that the $20 chip would make my computer 30 percent faster: all I had to do was remove the CPU and plug the V20 in its place. It seemed unbelievable to me — a magic chip that would instantly make my computer speedier.

I was nervous. I trusted Tim, but performing a brain transplant on my PC was scary. This computer was my baby, and if we messed up its motherboard or CPU, I would have killed my computer and therefore ruined my life. Nevertheless, we removed the PC's metal case and carefully pried out the 8088 with a flat-head screwdriver, then popped in the V20. The new brain worked like a charm: my PC was magically a little faster at everything.

But it was still not as fast as the PC AT in the back room at Dad's travel agency. That poor PC AT got to do three things all day. One: act as a dumb terminal to access the airline reservation system. Two: once a night, run the software to report ticket sales to the Airline Reporting Commission. Three: it spent the rest of its time with my dad playing a video poker simulation. Of course this was back in the days when people needed to go to a travel agency to get airline tickets, and before you could play poker online for real money.

Back in my bedroom, my XT wasn't limited to airline tickets and poker — I used it for all kinds of schoolwork, playtime, and teaching myself about programming. I spent a lot of time using the PC-Write word processor, which was one of the first shareware products ever. (Sorry: no, I didn't pay for it.) Dad bought me a 24-pin Epson dot matrix printer, which churned out papers throughout my high school and college years. Naturally, I also spent a lot of time playing games: I got pirated copies of graphical adventure games like Police Quest and Leisure Suit Larry. I went to Egghead Software and actually paid for a copy of Starflight, a space exploration game.

Although it had BASIC built in, this was the first computer that I didn't spend a significant amount of time programming in BASIC. With some help from books from the library, I started programming in Turbo Pascal and Turbo C. I taught myself to program in those languages, picking up bits from manuals, books, and computer magazines. I wasn't very good, but when college programming classes rolled around a few years later, I already had most of the concepts under my belt. I also tried using my PC to learn Prolog with the help of a book that I borrowed from the Thousand Oaks library. I liked the idea of being able to create artificially intelligent programs, which was supposed to be Prolog's forte. But, wow, Prolog's syntax seemed very different from the other languages I was learning — or maybe it just wasn't a very good book — and I gave it up.

PHONE LINE

The PC XT was amazing. But it was an island, unconnected to the outside world. I needed to get that PC online, so I could call bulletin board systems. This was a two-part process: getting a phone line of my own, then getting a modem. Both would require approval from Mom and Joe — but mostly Mom.

She wouldn't have it. She absolutely forbid that I get a modem for the Apple //c, but her resolve was beginning to weaken by the time I had the PC XT for a while. Plugging in with a modem concerned her for many reasons that now, as an adult, I can see were mostly legitimate — but don't tell her I said that. First of all, I would have to pay for the phone line, and that wasn't cheap.

By the time I was entering my junior year of high school, I was old enough to get a job — so it was agreed that if I got a job and could pay for the phone line myself, I could have it. I got the job and the phone line in 1987, but the modem would prove to be a long and ongoing battle with my mom. That took another year to get approved.

In April 1989, two months before I was to graduate high school, I had to write an essay for a composition class about a turning point in my life. The subject I choose just screams geek:

> *The first major turning point in my life was the acquisition my very own phone.*
>
> *Now, to the average person, the acquirement of seven little numbers means virtually nothing, save the ability to call girls and make dates. (I have no need for this.) Instead, my seven little numbers brought to my life a feeling of power, growth, and belonging.*
>
> *How could a Realistic DuoFone 202 and a Pac Bell general residence line, coupled with a DuoFone TAD-330 electronic answering device change a person's life? Very indirectly, in fact.*

It was with extreme reluctance that my mom allowed me to get the phone line. But she did, partly because she felt I had matured enough to cope with the responsibility, but mostly because she wanted me to get me off her back. But on August 13, 1987, the Pac Bell man came and went, leaving behind my very own 4-pin phone input, and forever changing my life.

On the first night of my line's existence, I spent many hours calling the operator, asking her to ring back my phone, thus proving to myself beyond a doubt that it did, in fact, exist. Twenty days later, the phone bill arrived.

Oh, my God.

There goes my allowance for the next three years. So much for maturity and handling responsibility. I'd have to get a job.

Within a week, I had acquired a position at Round Table Pizza. ...

It was the phone that had sent me down the road of responsibility: to find a job, make money, and pay the bills. It was the phone that helped me learn to deal with the world around me. It was the phone that brought me a sense of belonging.

From that meager job at Round Table, I reluctantly entered a more adult world: one in which money is everything, and the people are not always kind. But,

*whenever I felt low, I could always just pick up the
phone, and talk to a friend who cared. More than once, I
confronted a long-distance operator with my problems.
What would I do without Pacific Bell?*

*My little DuoFone will always have special significance
to me, as the gateway to my first major turning point.*

Some of the stuff in that essay was just hyperbole, B.S.,
and fluff to hit the required word count for the assignment.
I never bothered the operator with my problems, and I
knew within pennies what that first phone bill would total
before it landed in the mailbox. I did need to talk to girls,
I just didn't know how — I was a terrible nerd. But there
was some truth in what I wrote: the phone line *was* a big
deal for me. In addition to calling friends, I dipped my
toe in the waters of phone phreaking and free telephone
entertainment lines.

There were interesting numbers to call, such as dial-
a-joke lines, "comment lines," and conference lines. Set
up by telephone hobbyists, these numbers provided all
sorts of after-school entertainment possibilities. When you
called a comment line like REC407, you'd hear a cassette
tape which played on an endless loop: it might contain
little skits and funny songs, as well as voice recordings
previously left by other listeners. A comment line usually
had a corresponding input line, which was basically an
answering machine where people could leave messages,
which might be selected for use in the next comment line
recording. Many of the output line recordings from REC407

are available on the Web (home.recnet.com/te) and today I find them pretty terrible to listen to. Perhaps they haven't aged well, or maybe I haven't.

The guy who ran REC407, who went by the pseudonym Rich E. Calcom, occasionally held a call-in trivia contest called Dump Quiz. Contestants could call in and answer trivia questions, but if you answered incorrectly you were unceremoniously hung up on (or "dumped"). You were welcome to call in again for more trivia, if the lines didn't fill up with other contestants first.

Calcom also ran a conference line: you'd call in and be connected to two or three other people who had also called in. So at first I'd be talking with random strangers, but after awhile I got to know the regulars, and became a regular myself. Most of the other users were kids like me, maybe a few years older. A few creepy predator types hung out on the conference line occasionally, but mostly it was harmless fun talking to other young people.

Somewhere, I got a list of interesting 800 numbers to call. It included such exciting numbers as the White House press announcement line, where you could listen Ronald Reagan's weekly radio address. I called many of them, exploring the strange world of semi-interesting phone numbers that you could call for free.

I put the phone to profitable use, too. A company held a sweepstakes where you could call in, once an hour maximum, and leave your name and address for a chance to win fabulous prizes. I called before school, after school, and occasionally in the middle of the night if I woke up to use the bathroom. I called from the payphones at school during lunch hour. I must have entered that phone sweepstakes hundreds of times. When it was all over, I won a couple of little prizes including a Tom Petty CD, which was the first compact disc that I owned. It would be a year or so before I had a CD player to play it in.

I also called in to radio call-in contests. Sometimes I'd go to sleep with the clock radio on. With less competition for radio contests in the middle of the night (normal people were sleeping) I had a better chance of being the 10th caller. In exchange for interrupted sleep, I won weekend passes to Universal Studios.

Not too long after I got the phone line and the job at Round Table to pay for it, I received a phone bill that was much higher than it should have been. On the bill I found dozens of calls to pay-per-minute 976 numbers — calls which I didn't make. 976 numbers were used to talk to naughty girls. Naughty, expensive girls.

I called the phone company in a panic, and they said they'd look into it. They discovered that the neighbor across the street from us had tapped into my phone line — he could use my line from his house. I don't know for sure if he had a line of his own which had accidentally been tapped into my line by the phone company, or if the neighbor just grabbed a random wire pair for free sex line calls — but I have my suspicions. The phone company fixed the problem and reversed the charges.

The neighbor turned out to be my manager at Round Table. Crap. Every time he saw me in the following weeks he'd say something like "Still calling those sex lines, Kevin?" We both knew that he was in fact the pervert (and a thief). What a creep.

Round Table was a pretty good job: for the first few months, I made pizzas, washed dishes, and cleared tables. I had wanted the cashier job — it was generally regarded as the best job in the place, but the powers that be were happy with me in cooking and washing in the back. One day, there was an all-hands meeting to announce the restaurant had new owners effective immediately, but everything would be the same, don't you worry. My shift started immediately after that meeting. I brazenly walked up to the cash register and went to work, figuring that the new owners wouldn't know that that wasn't my usual job. My ploy worked, and from then on I was a regular at the register.

There were three or four arcade games at the pizza parlor — I played Cabal quite a bit on my breaks. During my senior year of high school, I started writing an essay, which was supposed to be humorous but fell significantly short of that goal, about behind-the-scenes secrets of the pizza place:

> *Video Games — People don't go to pizza places to eat pizza. They go to play video games and eat pizza between quarters. I have yet to understand peoples' fascination with video games. And would someone PLEASE explain to the two-year-olds that they aren't controlling the (&@(*! machine, and they're blocking the path to the bathroom!? Why are the little darlings so fascinated by getting the yellow dot to eat the blue*

dots, or speeding at 180 MPH through downtown L.A.?
Remember: these are the people who will be running
the country in thirty years. And driving on the 101
right behind you. And eating pizzas. And blue dots.

Jukebox — Don't waste your time. The jukebox has
a mind of its own and will go out of its way to NOT
play the selections that you choose. Your best bets are
to either choose songs that you don't want to hear, or
buy a cheap radio.

I also wrote a essay for English class titled "Method
For Creation and Preparation of Dynamic Circular Edible
Ethnic Foodstuff ... or, How To Make a Pizza." It's not worth
reading. Here's a particularly terrible sentence:

Toppings are generally regarded as the most important
part of the pizza. You may regard them (as do the
French) as the "pizza de resistance."

After a little more than a year at Round Table, I found
a better-paying job at Davis Research, a company that
conducted surveys over the phone. I didn't write any
humorous essays about that gig, because there wasn't much
humorous about it. I'd call and ask people their opinions
about the latest issue of L.A. Times Magazine, or about
their political preferences. The firm had a lot of clients, so
we were kept busy. Occasionally I'd call the They Might
Be Giants Dial-A-Song line between legitimate phone
calls. It was a long distance call to Brooklyn, New York,

but I took the Dial-A-Song motto to heart: "free when you call from work."

＊ ＊ ＊

While I was at work and school, an answering machine guarded my phone line. In retrospect, I don't know why I needed an answering machine at all, but I sure had fun with it. I used all of the audio tools at my disposal — cassette tape players, an old reel-to-reel tape recorder, and a borrowed sampling keyboard — to create crazy and inventive outgoing messages.

In one, I started in a calm voice, "Hello, this is Kevin. When you hear the tone, leave your message. I don't want to know who you are or the number to call you back at, but I do want to know what time you called." Then I started to yell: "What time is it? That's all I want to know! WHAT TIME IS IT?!"

So that was weird and confusing for the friends and family who called me. Next came the good part: I saved the confused incoming messages that callers left in response, then spliced them together to create a new outgoing message. "You're f&*(ed, Kevin. ... What is wrong with you? ... I don't even know what time it is ..." and so on.

I also dabbled in illegal uses of the phone line: making free long distance calls with calling card numbers that someone else had provided, and utilizing hacked voicemail boxes paid for by some company, somewhere. You might call it phone phreaking, but it wasn't. I was doing legally questionable stuff with the phone, but I wasn't figuring it out for myself. What I was doing was like what script kiddies do with computers today: just following directions provided by someone else to achieve an end. Not only was it wrong, but there was no art in it. Real phone phreaks (like Captain Crunch) were figuring out systems for themselves; I was just entering codes that I got from people that I met on the conference lines. Today, I'm not proud of those illegal phone activities — not only because it was wrong, but because it was too easy.

Luckily I didn't get caught, and luckily I didn't do much of that stuff. I had more interesting things to do with my time.

1200 BITS PER SECOND

Step one of Project Modem was complete: I had the phone line and was paying for it myself. Step two was getting Mom's approval for the modem itself. She said no, no, no. Her biggest concern: that I would start a nuclear war like that kid in WarGames.

Damn it. WarGames set back my goal of getting a modem, and finally getting online more than every other weekend at Dad's house, back by months. It was a great movie; still is. But Mom saw it too and was convinced that the Secret Service would come knocking at the door because of the mischief I would do online.

Apparently I was not the only one with this problem. While writing the section about Infocom and The New Zork Times, I found this letter in the summer 1984 issue:

Dear Duffy:
There's a girl in my Science class who I really have
a crush on. I invited her to my house to play Zork II
on my TI-99. We had a really good time, but then her
parents found out about it. They've seen "Wargames"
and think that all computer hackers are dangerous
criminals. What should we do?
                        —Not A Dangerous Criminal

Dear Not:
This is a common syndrome among parents. Explain
to them, in an intelligent and mature way, that you
are not going to blow up the world, and that Zork II
is a harmless and educational pastime. If this doesn't
work, get a lucrative job in the computer industry,
start your own high-tech company, attract millions
in venture capital, buy a huge estate in California,
take lots of world cruises, get elected to an important
government post, discover a cure for cancer, and write
several best-selling novels. After that, her parents
probably won't mind if she visits you to play Zork III.

After months of fruitless asking and pleading, the
summer before I was to be senior in high school I wrote
Mom a letter explaining why I wanted a modem. I wrote
the letter on June 22, 1988, which was probably about ten
seconds into summer vacation. She rejected the first version of the letter, sending it back to me for spelling and
grammar corrections.

Here's what I wrote,:

SUGGESTIONS BOX ..or..
LETTER TO THE EDITOR ..or..
COMPLAINTS DEPT.

Dear Mom,

Hi there. Official Document from the Teenage Seniors Association of my Room.

You seem rather bent on my not having a modem. And I really can't talk to you about this, because that's not something that you want to do.

It is very important to me that I can at least voice what I have to say, so that's what I'm doing.

As you undoubtedly know, I want to own a modem for my computer. This is not the evil, awful, mind-altering device that you may think it is. I promise, it will not cause my eyes to bulge out, my speech to stutter, nor will it make me listen to Iron Maiden (loudly). All that it will do is make me a happy person.

1) I just bought a stereo. Fine. It's a wonderful, neat, great, hi-tech, cool, good, etc. piece of equipment. Now I want a modem. (To be technical, I wanted a modem far before I mentioned a stereo. I seem to remember whining about this as a Freshman, if not before.) It

is not a crime to own two neat things. It is also no crime to buy them both within the space of two months.

2) Grades. As I have no doubt pointed out, my Junior year has ended. Great! My Sr. year will be much easier to handle, and my Jr. grades seemed to have turned out rather well. I'm happy with them. I managed to get all 48,004,012 projects done, including slideshow, ISP, history project (JFK), book report (Asimov), etc.. I am sure that adding a modem to my life will in no way hurt my grades next year. (As you'll recall, when I wanted an Apple //c 2-3 Christmases ago, the whole world was wondering: would Kevin's grades go down? No.) I know that I can balance school and leisure, as I am growing as a person, and in maturity. (Who writes this stuff?)

3) Job. Repeat: "I know I can balance work and leisure, as I am growing as a person, etc. etc."

4) Why do I need a &%@*@#(!! Modem, Anyway? Primarily, for fun. This is difficult to explain.. Uh, I get to use a modem while at Steve's, and it's great, but I'm not there often enough to really participate, (for instance, discussions that go on on different topics — I can't be in them because I'm not there long enough to be.) It's fun. Besides discussions, I can download (receive) programs to my computer.

That's good! In fact, in three cases when I was working on school assignments, a modem would most probably have saved me when I didn't have a word processor, or had erased my document files, etc. But mostly for fun.

5) Money. Not a lot. $140 max. Probably around $120. And I already have all I need to run it. The phone line. That's it. I have the software (program) to make it work. Don't need to spend more money. And one of the reasons I got the phone line was for running a modem. ("No, Kevin. Your Junior year is going to be rough. I don't want you getting a modem now. Maybe after this year.")

6) Pleading. Mom, this is something that is really important to me. It's like a hobby. I can't really translate it to something like you do...something you enjoy and do just for fun.

And I promise if i can get one, I will never talk to you about it and bug you. PLEASE re-think your reasons and consider what I have to say here. Thanks.

Remarkably, that letter did the trick.

With Mom's approval, I bought an internal modem (cheaper than an external modem, but lacking the cool blinky lights). A whopping 1200 bits per second. With my own phone line, I could tie up the phone all night downloading games.

I can't remember buying the modem or installing it, but I do remember hour upon happy hour using QMODEM to dial BBSes. There were lots of BBSes in the 818 area code, which I was able to dial for the first time.

The PC-based BBSes that I could call in the Valley seemed like a different world from the Atari-based BBSes that I was familiar with from my dad's house, way over in the 213 area code. The local, free, calling area was still limited to a certain distance from your house, so the BBSes that I could call from Agoura were a completely different set than the ones I could dial from Dad's. Luckily, the 818 area code was a hotbed of BBSes.

Also, the PC BBSes had some features that made them an exciting new experience, compared to the Atari boards I was used to. Now I could see text in 80 columns instead of 40, and in color. And the 1200 BPS modem was four times faster than Dad's Atari modem.

I picked a new handle for my online adventures. "Kevin Komix" was feeling like an old name, and was definitely a handle that was shared by Dad and me. My new alias, "cfa waffle?" was for me alone. It was short for "care for a waffle?" (The phrase didn't have any particular significance. I took it from a line of dialogue in an episode of Family Ties.) Years later, I shortened it to just "waffle" for access to Unix systems and Internet sites: I still use the waffle alias from time to time.

One bulletin board that I frequented was called The Federation. It was a warez board, always good for downloading quality stolen software. That board held a monthly

ANSI art contest, where users could create low-res computer art. Although the PC's ANSI graphics set was completely different than the Atari's, I used my Kevin Komix skills to create some fun ANSI art screens, winning the $25 prize a couple of times. One of my winning entries was an animation of Santa coming down the chimney.

Another favorite 818 area code bulletin board was a little system called Your Guess Is As Good As Mine. The YGIAGAM sysop and I became friends, and talked on the phone often, though we never met in person. He made me co-sysop on his board, a position which made me feel important but included no actual authority whatsoever. I had fun on that board creating amusing surveys for the other users to fill out.

My favorite PC bulletin boards — including both Federation and YGIAGAM — ran on software called WWIV. My fellow online denizens had a lot of discussions about whether that was supposed to be pronounced "double U double U eye vee" or "World War Four" or something else.

Some of the BBSes were part of FIDOnet, which was an interconnected system of BBSes spanning the world. You could write a public or private message on your local BBS in California, and that night your message would be sent to the next FIDOnet BBS in the chain. The next night, it could get sent to a couple more systems even farther away. If someone replied to your message, it would take an equal amount of time for their message to wend its way back to your home BBS. It was not a speedy way to communicate, but it was an early taste of global e-mail a few years before I got real access to the Internet.

Many years later, in 1993, I wrote an article for Online Access magazine about FidoNet. According to that article, FidoNet was created in 1984; it was four years old by the time I finally had a modem. I could have gotten in on the ground floor if I had a modem earlier — oh, Mom! Why couldn't you have caved sooner?

Danny and I spent a lot of time modifying the WWIV BBS source code, adding all sorts of features like a currency system. Our hacks didn't make it on to an actual, online BBS that people called in to — I don't think Danny ever shared our modifications; they were just for our own amusement. (Although a few months later, a new version of WWIV added an official currency system and some of the other features that we had created independently.)

I stayed over at Dan's house one night for an epic, all-night WWIV source code hacking session. We prepared for the all-night programming fest by watching The Last Starfighter on his dad's videodisc player — the player flipped the disc automatically at the halfway point, so you could watch the entire movie without getting up from the couch! We were living in the future. Then came the programming, where we sat side-by-side at his PC and discussed the best way to create a feature or implement a function. By 2 or 3 in the morning, I was dead, lying on the carpet and begging for sleep. But Danny was a programming machine, and pushed through the night. In the morning his mom made us pancakes.

PRODIGY

Besides calling BBSes, I got an account on Prodigy. Prodigy was a national online service that charged a flat monthly fee. Up until that point, all of the big online services, like CompuServe, charged per hour. My dad had a "Compu$erve" account but hardly ever used it: it cost $6 an hour! When you're making just over minimum wage making pizza — $3.35 an hour in 1988 — $6 an hour is too much. Prodigy cost $9.95 a month, a price that I could handle.

Prodigy was the first national online service to use a graphical interface. They were kind of kludgy, grayscale (at least on my computer) graphics — but real graphics that were a step up from the blocky ANSI graphics that BBSes provided. Another cool feature was that you could have several sub-accounts on each account. My dad used one, and for a while my high school economics class used another to look up stock prices. We started the year with a class challenge to see who could make the most (simulated) money trading stocks. But some students cheated the system, "buying" stocks at the price listed in the morning paper, only after checking Prodigy to find out which stocks had risen that day.

Almost ten years later, my knowledge about Prodigy caused a heated argument between some of the world's best-known geeks. It was 1998: I wrote some trivia questions for the Quiz Bowl, which was an annual geek trivia contest and fundraiser for The Computer Museum in Boston, Massachusetts. The quiz pitted West Coast geeks (that year they were Marc Andreessen, Scott Cook, Bill Krause, Michael Slade, and Denise Caruso) against East Coast geeks (Seth Godin, Walt Mossberg, Ken Wasch, Mike Zisman, and Robert Ziff).

One of the questions that I wrote, which was about Prodigy, caused the commotion. John Ratzenberger, the guy who played Cliff Clavin on Cheers, asked the question: "The Prodigy online service began as venture between two large corporations. One of them was IBM. Who was the other partner?" Marc Andreessen buzzed in and got the answer that I expected: Sears. His team was declared correct. But the East Coast team immediately raised a fuss, shouting that there was a third company involved: CBS. For a moment, the host said that East Coast team was right, West was wrong, which caused more arguments and yelling. So he threw out the question and asked John Ratzenberger to ask a new question, a "less controversial" one. (You can watch the whole dramatic thing at www.archive.org/details/Computer98, about 24 minutes in.)

If you're curious about the correct answer — well, it's complicated. The East Coast players had a valid point: CBS *was* involved as one of the three (not two) corporations that, in 1984, founded Trintex, the company that would become Prodigy. However, CBS left the venture in 1986, a full two years before the Prodigy online service was launched in test markets. All in all, it just wasn't a good question for the Quiz Bowl.

I used Prodigy for a year or two, but it was an easy service for a techie to outgrow. I cancelled my account right before I moved up to Northern California for college — Prodigy didn't have a local dial-up number there.

THE SUMMER BEFORE COLLEGE

Mom was divorcing Joe as I was finishing high school. She timed it perfectly, I think more out of convenience for me than anything else.

I did the pomp and circumstance of the graduation ceremony. That evening, it was grad night at Disneyland. Grad night, a multi-school graduation party, started at around 10 at night and continued until the wee hours of the morning. My friends and I went on lots of rides. I got to see Information Society play a set at the Tomorrowland Terrace. The bus left Disneyland at 3 or 4 a.m., headed back to Calabasas High. I was in my bed in Agoura at maybe 6 a.m., and slept until 10.

When I got up, it was time. Mom had already packed up her stuff. I put the last of my things in a box and put it all in the car, gave Joe a goodbye hug, and then Mom and I left that house for good. She had gotten an apartment in Simi Valley. I drove to my dad's house to stay with him for the summer before college.

All in all, it made for a weird day.

(I did go back to that house in Agoura once, many years later. I went there with my wife and daughter to see the old neighborhood. The owners were home, and were gracious enough to let us inside to look around. The new owner was using my old room as an office. It had a bunch of computers in it, which was as it should be. I couldn't get over how small the house seemed, my room especially. I was a lot bigger than I was when I lived there, and the house seemed to have shrunk in inverse proportion.)

Back at Dad's beach house in 1989, my IBM PC replaced the Atari 800 on the desk, and Dad and I had a nice summer together. I got a crappy job making phone calls soliciting donations for a political party, and spent my free time volunteering at the local cable TV station, helping to produce local access interview shows that weren't of interest even to the locals.

When mid-August came, I went to the post office and mailed a lot of my stuff to myself in Arcata, California, home of Humboldt State University. We stuffed the rest of my things into Mom's car, and drove 700 miles north.

PART 2

CHAPTER 8
HUMBOLDT STATE

Mom and I unloaded my things into my off-campus studio apartment, with a shared bathroom and communal kitchen. My major was journalism, with an emphasis on news and editorial.

I had chosen Humboldt State because it was small (about 7,300 students at the time) and as far away as possible, while still remaining in the state of California, which kept registration fees low. HSU is at the northern end of the state — it's a rural area, relative to the Los Angeles city sprawl, blanketed in fog and redwood forests.

The first student I met there — literally, the first stranger that I met at college — was a huge nerd, became my best friend, and is still one of my closest friends today. Mitch was typing away at a keyboard in a public area, on some kind of computer that I wasn't familiar with. I walked up and asked him what kind of computer that was. He patiently explained that it wasn't actually a computer, it was a terminal connected to a Unix computer elsewhere on campus. A new door opened, a door to the world of the Unix operating system and eventually the Internet.

That night, I went to a bookstore and bought a book about Unix. I read it as quickly as I could. My first day of college hadn't even started and I was already learning interesting new things. Mitch set me up with an account on the AT&T 3B2/400, a minicomputer that he took care of because no one else on campus paid any attention to it. There were other minicomputers and mainframes on campus that I'd get access to eventually, but the 3B2 and it's Unix-y goodness became my home base at HSU. Partly because I quickly became comfortable with its Unix operating system, and partly because the system administrator was Mitch, and he let me do whatever I wanted with it.

My IBM PC and my Oingo Boingo poster were key features of the $200/month studio apartment my freshman year.

Beyond a quick tour as part of a computer class, I was never allowed into the school's mainframe lab — although I did score accounts on as many of the machines as I could. They had a Control Data Cyber 830 and a PDP 11/70, and other big iron monsters, in a big, loud room with a raised floor for easy access to wiring.

When I first got to college, none of the computers on campus were directly connected to the Internet; they were on BITnet, a network of university computers that didn't offer all of the features of the full Internet. My e-mail address was kevin@calstate.BITNET. I started exploring the world of global e-mail services, Listservs, and Usenet.

Usenet was the message boards of the Internet before the Web. Usenet still exists, but it pales in popularity compared to its former glory before Web-based forums blossomed. It is made up of thousands of topical groups, called newsgroups. The other popular way to have discuss specific topics was on Listservs, or e-mail discussion groups. I downloaded a list of all the public e-mail mailing lists — it was long — and rather than use my own printer, sent it to be printed by the high-speed line printer in the school's mainframe lab. The next day I went to pick up my printout — it had to be at least 1,000 pages of green-bar computer paper. To my surprise, no one in the lab flinched at my massive print job. I knew I was going to love my time at college.

Before too long the school was upgraded to a full-fledged Internet connection. I dove into FTP: downloading endless amounts of public domain software from Simtel20, a software archive that was, for some strange reason, housed at New Mexico's White Sands Missile Range.

I also explored the possibilities of Telnet, a tool that lets you connect to and login to far-away computers. No longer was I limited to computers in California. I discovered the ability to Telnet into the Cleveland Freenet, a popular public system at Case Western Reserve University (which happened to have a thriving Atari users forum, bonus!) Mitch showed me how to find computer systems at MIT with accounts owned by Richard Stallman, a fellow who didn't believe in passwords — so anyone could use his accounts which always had the username "rms" and password "rms". There was so much to explore.

(Stallman was the instigator of the Free Software Foundation and the GNU Project, the software tools that would become a key component of Linux. Years later I would interview him for a computer magazine article, and man, did he have strong opinions. For one, he wouldn't agree to an interview unless I called the operating system GNU Linux in the article — even through everyone just called it Linux — because he felt that the latter didn't give proper credit to the GNU Project.

I could use my PC to dial in to the school's computers from my little apartment, but that was limited to the speed of my 1200 BPS modem. The computer labs on campus provided high-speed access. There were labs all over the place: from a basement room filled with dumb terminals to labs loaded with Mac IIs and speedy PCs. After I was at Humboldt State for a year or two, one of the science buildings installed a lab filled with Sun Sparcstations — speedy, graphical Unix workstations that were administrated by a bearded, proto-typical Unix god named Don. Don wouldn't tolerate any shenanigans on his workstations, but also he didn't seem to mind that I wasn't taking any science classes and had no official business in his lab. (Mitch, an astrophysics major, seemed to have nothing but science classes.)

Another machine that I had no business playing with was the NeXT computer in the library. As far as I knew, HSU had just the one, and it was locked away in tiny room in the library where no one ever seemed to use it. I talked my way in and got to use it once or twice. It had pretty graphics and amazing multi-tasking capabilities.

I also found a lab on campus filled with IBM PS/2 computers. It should be clear by now that I loved computers; loved to learn about them and explore their capabilities. But I had never found a computer as uninteresting as the PS/2. They weren't sexy on the outside or the inside, they couldn't do hardware multitasking like the NeXT or the Amiga. They were brand new, but just ran DOS like my XT. There was nothing alluring about these machines: it's like IBM methodically leeched the fun out of computers. A whole room filled with those dull grey bricks. It really was disappointing to discover, for the first time, a computer that wasn't interesting to me. In retrospect, perhaps I was like an art lover realizing that he didn't have to like all kinds of art. Or maybe those PS/2s just sucked.

Being part of the college universe got me access to other machines in the California State University system.

I got an account on the CSU's central Cyber system, and another on a Unix box at San Diego State University, at the other end of the state. I didn't have legitimate needs for any of those accounts, but I did have a desire to explore and a signature from a professor, and that's all that was necessary.

Back in the closet that housed the 3B2, Mitch compiled a game called Nethack and got me hooked on it. Despite low-tech ASCII graphics and no sound, Nethack was and still is the best computer game ever. (For more info, see www.TheGreatestGameYouWillEverPlay.com.) I've been playing it on and off since 1989, and have never come close to winning, but it's still fun. I also discovered The Purity Test, a quiz that served as a veritable checklist of things for a college student to do. Or rather, a list of things other college students were doing as I spent my time pondering why the PS/2 was boring.

College life provided plenty of nerdy things to do off campus, too. Mitch and I spent many evenings at Sharkey's Arcade, feeding tokens into Hard Drivin', Cyberball, and Rolling Thunder. Tokens at Sharkey's Arcade were five for a dollar, but were the same size and weight as the tokens for the photocopier at the college library, which were only ten cents each. I invested heavily in copier tokens. We also hung out at Tiffany's Garden for Children, a little arcade-restaurant that was supposed to be an after-school hang-out for little kids, but was a perfectly suitable after-school hangout for us big kids too. The Arcata theater had great midnight shows — Monty Python, Rocky Horror, sick and twisted animation festivals, and concert films. It's a wonder that I got any schoolwork done.

HAM RADIO

In addition to going to classes and geeking out with Unix, I earned an amateur radio license during my freshman year. My dad had been a ham radio operator, and Mitch was also, so I bought a book and some Morse code practice cassette tapes and studied like crazy. Decoding the dits and dahs of Morse code was not a skill that came easily to me: I barely squeaked by the (allegedly) easy five words-per-minute that was required to earn the Novice license. Upgrading to the next-level Technician license a few weeks later wasn't a problem: that just required a multiple-choice test. For me, memorizing facts was much easier than interpreting Morse code. The next level, the General class license, presented another hurdle, requiring the ability to understand Morse code at a speedy 13 words per minute. I had to take that test several times before finally passing the General exam.

Although there were two more classes of amateur radio license available at the time, I stopped there. The Advanced class required a huge test filled with complex electronics and antenna topics that I didn't understand — and that would only lead to the Extra class and its insurmountable 25-words-per-minute Morse code test. General was good enough, and provided all the operating privileges that I needed anyway.

(In 2007, the FCC dropped the Morse code requirements for all amateur radio licenses: all that is necessary now is to learn the answers to the multiple-choice tests. Although at the time there seemed to be a lot of people with the opinion "I had to suffer through learning Morse code — so should you!" in the end the change was good for the hobby, significantly lowering the bar to get on the air at a time where widespread access to the Internet was putting a serious dent in the number of ham radio operators. In part because of the shift away from Morse code, at the end of 2011, the number of ham radio operators in the United States hit an all-time high.)

I bought a Kenwood "handie talkie," a walkie talkie that worked on the 2-meter amateur radio band. It was portable — I often took it to school, on vacations, everywhere. Compared to the tiny HTs that are available now, the thing seems monstrous, like comparing the first cell phones in the 1980s to the iPhone. Of course, this was before cell phones were ubiquitous, and the portable radio came in handy one day when my geology class was on a field trip. After a stop in the middle of nowhere looking at an Alquist-Priolo zone, the bus wouldn't start. I grabbed the radio from my backpack and let the professor use the autopatch — a radio-to-telephone interconnection — to call for another bus.

Ham radio also melded with my computing hobby: I bought a packet radio modem, a gadget that let my PC talk to other computers over the radio (instead of over the phone line like with a regular modem). Packet radio delivered a new world of radio-based BBSes to explore, plus I could try to capture data from satellites that passed overhead. Occasionally a space shuttle mission would include a astronaut who was a ham: I could see them sending packet radio messages to other Earth-bound hams, but my antenna wasn't good enough so they never received my signal.

Later, when I had a car, I had a personalized license plate with my ham radio callsign, KC6GWQ — advertising my nerdiness everywhere I drove.

VIDEO CONCEPTS

I went back down to Southern California to stay with Dad for the summer after my freshman year. He was still managing the travel agency at the mall, so it made sense for me to get a job at the mall too. I really wanted a position at the computer software store: they had software for every system — PCs, Macs, Amiga, Atari ST. Best of all, they had a policy of letting employees borrow software to use at home, then re-shrinkwrap it for sale. I think they figured that the more employees knew about the software, by using it in their off-time, the better salespeople they would be. I figured that it would be a great way to get free copies of all the software I wanted.

The owner of the software shop seemed to like me but said there weren't any positions available. I tried to make it clear that I really wanted the job and knew my stuff, but he wasn't hiring. So I walked two stores over and was hired by Video Concepts, a chain that sold TVs and stereo equipment. It was a commissioned sales job, with a guaranteed per-hour minimum that was only slightly over minimum wage. I was a terrible salesman. Most of the time my commissions barely squeaked past the minimum hourly rate. I discovered that I hated pushing people to buy things. I hated upselling them to the extended warranty. Can I interest you in a Video Concepts credit card? My philosophy was to tell people the specs, explain why one TV was better or worse than another, and let the shopper decide. In the end I don't think this was what the company really wanted, but pushy sales wasn't my thing. It still isn't. I hope it never is.

The job had its perks: there were all sorts of gadgets to play with and it was fun to blast music really loudly from really nice speakers (usually before the mall opened, but we could get away with it during open hours in the name of customer demonstrations). The store sold Amiga 500s and a pathetic Tandy PC clone, although I don't think we sold a single computer in the summer that I worked there. People just didn't go to a TV and stereo store to buy a computer. And even if they did, we didn't stock peripherals or any decent software.

A few weeks into the job, the man from the software shop came back, and pleaded with me to quit Video Concepts and work at his software store. But he had had his chance — I stuck it out at Video Concepts out of a sense of obligation. I had made a commitment to work there all summer.

※ ※ ※

As the fall term approached, I headed back to Humboldt State, and rented a room at my friend Mitch's place. Mitch lived in a house in Blue Lake, the next town over from the university and a short drive to school. The house had been his great-grandmother's until she died, and it hadn't been redecorated in any significant way since she passed. So, Mitch was living in a world of gold shag carpet, pink walls, and a multitude of ceramic elephant figurines. It was kind of terrifying, but kind of awesome.

We set up our computers — his Mac Plus, my PC XT — in the little attic room that had been Great-Grandma's sewing room. We called the room The Bridge, after the control center on the Starship Enterprise. Setting up The Bridge presented technical hurdles. The house, built in 1948, didn't have grounded, three-prong electrical outlets. The house only had one phone line, and that line only had one modular jack (where Great-Grandma's special medical alert phone used to connect). I needed special dispensation from the landlord, Mitch's dad, to add a second line (for my modem). Even once that was connected, the phone switch for the whole town of Blue Lake didn't really support DTMF (Touch-Tone) dialing. You could use your Touch-Tone phone, then you could hear the switch "click click click," re-sending the numbers as pulse dialing signals. Keep in mind this was 1990 — many cities made the switch to Touch-Tone in the 1970s.

Once we had The Bridge all set up, I found that the little, uninsulated attic room was freezing cold in the winter and sweltering the summer. Despite that, we had a great time working on school stuff, playing computer games, and doing programming projects in there.

One of the things I did there, that November: I broke the Internet *for all of Europe* for a few hours. I was hanging out on a sex-related Usenet newsgroup — hey, I was in college, and having sex sounded like a really good idea. I had downloaded a large batch of text files, an archive of a sex discussion and advocacy mailing list. It was easy to send the collection to whoever asked for it, so I offered on Usenet to e-mail it to anyone who wanted it. People from all over the world asked for the files, and I e-mailed them to whoever asked. A few hours later I received a livid e-mail from a network administrator in London, which was the gateway for Internet communications for all of Europe. He said I had single-handedly clogged the intercontinental Internet link with smut. There was no room for actual, non-sex-related traffic. The overseas link was probably only 56 kbits per second back then, very easy to saturate. Sorry guys.

Saturday night at the house was Star Trek night. We would have a gaggle of our nerdy friends over to eat pizza and watch Star Trek: The Next Generation.

One week, I went down to Santa Cruz, California to hang out with Danny, who was studying at U.C. Santa Cruz. For some reason it was a few days when Danny had classes but I didn't. During the day when he was in class, I relaxed in his dorm room and played games on his computer — I played a lot of Lemmings on his Amiga. In the evenings, Danny and his dorm friends and I hung out and watched movies. Here's what I ate that week: chips and salsa. When

I arrived, Danny bought a gigantic, industrial sized bag of corn chips and an equally impressive tub of Pace salsa. In grand college student tradition, I didn't have money for food, and though Danny was eating in the school cafeteria, he didn't have enough food points to feed me too. I scored half a sandwich here and there, but the majority of my sustenance that week was chips and salsa. I still can't stand the smell of Pace salsa.

At the end of my sophomore year, I was feeling ready to live without a housemate again (and, perhaps, without so many ceramic elephants), so I moved out of Mitch's house and into a one-bedroom apartment walking distance from campus. But I would be back.

GIRLS

I had three girlfriends in college. Or ever, actually.

The first was Beth, a beautiful, artistic girl who was a terrible starter girlfriend. Beth brought drama. First, her mom was into me. That was awkward. Skinny, nerdy, new-to-college Kevin had some existential angst from wanting to sleep with a woman whose mom wanted to sleep with me. Second, Beth had a boyfriend. They were living together — they were practically married. She eventually left him for me, but he didn't give her up easily. There was months of drama. Once, he broke into my (well, Mitch's) house to find Beth and I in bed together. He had ridden his unicycle six miles from Arcata to Blue Lake to break into the house. *He rode a unicycle. Six miles.* After a morning of yelling and angst and crying, I was so — I don't know what I was, a nice guy? stupid? — that I drove her, him, and the unicycle back to campus.

Needless to say, that relationship didn't work out. Beth dumped me and went back to him.

Girlfriend number two was Kim. I met Kim online in July 1991, through the alt.personals Usenet newsgroup, making her the first intersection of technology and females since my video-game playdate in elementary school. She described herself as a red-headed skater chick, which (surprisingly) is what she turned out to be. She was a student living in Southern California. We spent some time together that summer, but we were geographically undesirable for each other. Things were going well enough, but I broke up with her when it looked like I had a chance with girl number three.

Girl number three was Peace, and she would become my wife. As I was starting my junior year, I had signed up for a shift as a DJ at the college radio station, KRFH. Peace was the station manager.

I didn't know it then, but Peace had geek cred. When she was younger, she had a VIC-20 computer which her dad had won in a promotion at work. She recalls: "Since I knew more about computers than anyone else in the house, I got to choose the equipment. I chose a cassette drive instead of the disk drive, because you could get cassette tapes anywhere; who had ever heard of that disk drive thing?" She had taken summer-school Apple // programming classes, and still had the card that proclaimed her proficiency as a BASIC programmer (level 2). So I'm sure you can clearly see why Peace was the girl for me.

The day that I met Peace's mom for the first time, we all played Scrabble, and I played the word *erection*. Peace was mortified, but I couldn't pass up the 50-point bonus.

COLLEGE NEWSPAPER AND RADIO

As part of my journalism major, I spent lot of time helping to create student-run media.

The Lumberjack, the newspaper at Humboldt State, was a high-tech operation. Rows of Macs lined the desks, where writers could type their stories. Editors would lay out the pages on huge two-page CRT screens, then print the pages on a LaserWriter printer. The process wasn't completely digital, though. We still had to endure paste-up, using wax to stick the printed sheets to the newsprint templates. This was just about the state of the art for newspaper publishing. The photography process was still low-tech. As one of the paper's photographers, I spent hours at various campus and community events with a 35mm camera in hand — war protests, the launch of a new power plant, election night — and more hours processing the negatives in the darkroom. Then, I'd make a print which another student would use to create, via a PMT (photomechanical transfer) machine, a halftone version that would reproduce correctly on newsprint. The year I graduated was the year the paper started experimenting with Adobe Photoshop.

The student-run radio station, KRFH, Radio Free Humboldt, was not a high-tech, state-of-the art operation. Of the school's two radio stations, this was the low-rent district — it wasn't broadcast over the air, but via carrier current. That is, you could only hear it if your radio was plugged into a power outlet in certain areas on campus, which carried the signal. The little studio was located in the basement of the journalism department building, complete with turntables, a CD player, and cart players for playing commercials.

There were only a few listeners. Sometimes, as far as I could tell, there were no listeners, which really made me feel like I had creative freedom in my program. All of us DJs did — the mix of music at KRFH was eclectic, for sure. One semester, I called my program Difficult Listening Hour. Another semester, I aired the Dr. Demento show. The program arrived weekly on two LP records, with one long track on each side. The station could air the program for free as long as we played the whole thing, complete with commercials.

Being on the radio station staff provided me access to the school's audio studio, where I had endless fun creating silly commercials and public service announcements. There was nothing digital there — the editing facility consisted of a reel-to-reel tape recorder and a razor blade. To make an edit, you would use the razor to cut out the portion of audio tape that you wanted removed, then use a bit of cellophane tape to re-assemble the audio tape. The idea of editing audio with razors and tape sounds so archaic now — that's some serious old-school geek cred. One weekend, Peace and I used the editing room to create a series of PSAs called "Songs Not To Sing To Your Lover's Penis" — which included "Is That All There Is?" and "Grow For Me."

Radio classes weren't only about goofing around in the editing booth. In 1991, former HSU professor Alann Steen, who had been held hostage for years in Lebanon, was freed. I created a piece for the radio about the topic, and it won an award from the Society of Professional Journalists. Also, as part of a broadcast news class, we produced a five-minute daily news program which we read on air. We did our best, and it was good practice — but with an audience in the tens (if we were lucky) it wasn't really the end of the world if we screwed up. Which we did. One day my friend Gigi was overcome with a giggling fit while reading the day's news. I pushed her out of the studio and took over. The day that Dr. Seuss died, I wrote that news as a rhyming poem:

He died today at 87
He's now in Whoville, or Lorax heaven
My childhood would have been no use
without the prose of Dr. Seuss

I also did some volunteer work on the big-time campus radio station, KHSU. Unlike KRFH, KHSU had an actual transmitter and a professional studio. It played nationally syndicated shows from National Public Radio as well as local programming. It was broadcast to, and listened to by, the whole county, not just a few students on campus. Most of my volunteer time was spent babysitting the booth during our taped broadcasts of national shows. For instance, some engineer would record The Thistle & Shamrock from a satellite feed onto reel-to-reel tape. During my shift I would do the top-of-the hour station identification, then read the sponsor information ("Finnish Country Sauna and Tubs and Cafe Mokka, located at 5th and J streets in Arcata, featuring traditional sauna cabins, private outdoor hot tubs, a European coffee house, and a frog pond in an enchanted forest." I must have read that blurb many times to still remember it verbatim today) then start the tape. If it was a Friday afternoon, I got to insert the Dr. Science cart and play a funny clip.

That was how I spent most of my time in the studio. Occasionally, though, some DJ who had a show of their own would need a fill-in, and when they did I would jump at the opportunity to be a substitute disc jockey and program music myself. I was low man on the volunteer totem pole, so this was rare. One time, though, there was a need for a last-minute substitute DJ for the late-night rap show. I went to the studio at 11 on a Friday or Saturday night, and needed to fill the air with two hours of rap music. I knew *nothing* about rap music, but that wouldn't stop me — stacks of rap albums and CDs were kept in the music library adjacent to the studio. I had heard the rap show that I was filling in for — they played some raunchy, language-filled music. This was my opportunity to do the same! I knew the rules: the FCC said that "safe harbor hours" started after 10 p.m. — children wouldn't been listening to the radio at that hour, so the restrictions against what you could say and play on the radio were looser than during the day. So I used my two hours on the air to play the lewdest, nastiest, profanity-filled rap that I could find in the station's library.

The next Monday morning I was back on campus, walking to class. A fellow KHSU DJ came running up to me saying that I needed to go talk to the programming director *now*. The management was not happy with my programming choices. I didn't know that there had been a meeting just a few days earlier, in which the management had told the regular DJs in no uncertain terms that naughty music was not appropriate on the station at any hour. I had clearly missed that meeting. I was not asked to fill in for absent DJs again.

Ironically, Peace hosted a weekly rap show over at KRFH.

LAMBDAMOO

One of the wonders of the Internet back in the day was multi-user dungeons, more commonly called MUDs. These were the Internet's first MMORPGs: text-based worlds where you could explore, talk with other players, and go on quests. I had dabbled with several MUDs — my girlfriend Beth's mom was really into them — but none of the explore-the-cave, kill-the-dragon games were very interesting to me. (Some people were *really* into them — there were stories of college kids who were addicted to MUDs, forsaking classes and real-life friendships to live in their text-based fantasy worlds.)

Then I discovered a particular MUD called LambdaMOO, and I was hooked. Not hooked like forsaking class and friends and eating — but it was a different kind of MUD that appealed to me. The interesting thing about LambdaMOO was that anyone could program it: you could create rooms, link them together, then populate those rooms with objects that people could use. Playing a dragon-filled fantasy game that someone else built was boring, but creating games and other things for other people to use never got dull. LambdaMOO combined two of my favorite skills, writing and programming. My username was waffle (still is — I've still got the account, though I log in only occasionally).

The first thing I created was "Carla the llama," a pet llama that you could feed using its special bag of llama food. Later, I created a pizza parlor, complete with a jukebox and pizza delivery guy, a Scrabble board where up to four people could play, and versions of ELIZA and some other games from the Basic Computer Games books.

In case you're wondering what MOOcode looks like, here's a bit of code from Carla the llama's bag of llama chow:

```
#11527:feed   any (with/using) this
  if (!valid(dobj))
    player:tell("\"", dobjstr, "\" is not valid.");
  elseif (dobj.location != player.location &&
dobj.location != player &&
    (this.location != player.location && this.
location != player))
    player:tell("I don't see that here.");
  elseif (this.amount == 1)
    player:tell("You'll have to fill it first:
its empty.");
  else
    player:tell(dobj.name, " munches happily on
the llama feed.");
```

```
    dobj:tell(player.name, " feeds you some
llama feed. Yum!");
    player.location:announce _ all _ but({dobj,
player}, player.name, " feeds ",
      dobj.name, " some llama feed!");
    this.amount = this.amount - 1;
  endif
```

I also built word-wrapping for LambdaMOO:

```
A couple of the things that I created f
or LambdaMOO were pretty important for t
he community. When I started using the sy
stem, there was no word wrap - words wo
uld just break in the middle at the end
of each line, which makes it really har
d to read. The worst part was when I wa
s using these particular terminals on camp
us, which didn't wrap to a new line when th
e cursor reached the edge of the screen. In
stead, the letters just disappeared off t
he edge of the screen, which made the gam
e unplayable.
```

So I built a word-wrap function, which would nicely wrap text between words instead of in the middle of them. The wizards (the folks in charge) loved it and the function was quickly rolled out to all the users. I also wrote Mr. Spell, a spell checker (and had an interesting few days trying to populate it with 25,000 words from online word lists). Mr. Spell was also integrated into MOO's core software.

For a while I published the Lambda MOOspaper, a weekly roundup of news from around the virtual community. So it's fair to say that I was pretty involved with LambdaMOO during college and for a while after I graduated. I made a lot of friends, watched a lot of drama unfold, and enjoyed the community.

CHAPTER 9
FREELANCING

As I neared the end of my college career, it was time to figure out what I was going to do next — what my career would be. When I started college, I thought that I might want to eventually be a newspaper reporter or perhaps a photojournalist, but by now I had realized that I didn't want to do either of those jobs. Journalism and writing still appealed to me, but so did computers. I thought perhaps I could write for computer magazines — to be a part of the publications that I had been reading since I was little.

I could be a technology writer, at least until I got a real job. There hadn't been any classes in the HSU journalism curriculum on freelancing, so I'd have to figure it out for myself. I decided to ask an expert: I wrote a letter to John C. Dvorak, a prolific tech columnist whose work appeared in many computer magazines. I don't remember exactly what my letter said, other than asking for his advice on becoming a professional writer. On Valentine's Day 1991, he wrote a letter back:

> *Well, at least you figured out the game early. J [journalism]-schools and J-majors are designed to create a cookie cutter writer who is good for little more than writing straight news and getting three quotes. ... Also, journalism courses seldom stress or even discuss the importance of "voice" in writing. Voice is bad for a reporter. If you want to make money as a magazine or book writer — voice is everything. This is handled as a "secret" in J-school. I'm always amazed that someone can come out of J-school and become a famous writer. The hit ratio is very low, so they must be doing something wrong. ...*

> *As far as I'm concerned the key is the ability to explain things without being boring and to describe things in interesting ways. Computer and technical magazines are a great opportunity. They pay well and can't find enough people who know what they're talking about. If you can write a simple sentence with a little flair, you can get published. I don't know what else to tell you but to get out of journalism if you want to be a writer. I recommend history. History is one of the few academic disciplines that doesn't make you develop a screwball lexicon (like sociology, for example.) So you can practice writing in your style and using your language. ...*

If you want to be a writer you might have to sell insur-
ance for a few years before you get the opportunity to
do it full-time. I'd say that it's worth the wait if you
can handle it.

Last. I was told this when I was a kid and believed it
then and believe it now. Accept the following as fact:
If you want to be a writer then you'll be one.

I took some of John's advice — I continued to develop
my writer's voice. I passed on another big part of his advice:
I didn't switch away from the journalism major; I didn't
even consider it. But I was grateful for his advice, and that
he had taken the time to write that letter.

Another famous journalist helped me to get my first
paid writing gig, a few months before I graduated.

Jacques Leslie was (and still is) a big-time journalist.
He had been a correspondent for the L.A. Times during the
Vietnam War. In 1992, he was hanging around LambdaMOO
doing research for an article about MUDs. We spent some
time chatting over several days as I showed him around the
MOO and we talked about the community. I told him that
I was close to getting my B.A. in journalism and wanted to
break into writing about computers. He suggested freelance
writing, and gave me the contact information for the editor
of Microtimes, a computer magazine.

I e-mailed that editor, and she gave me an assignment,
just like that. I promised to have the article to her in a week,
but stayed up late and e-mailed her the finished article the

next day. The article, titled "Find Your Friends and E-Mail Your Enemies," explained how to find out people's e-mail addresses using a variety of arcane online tools. Microtimes paid me $200 for the article. I was giddy, a published free-lance writer before I even had a college diploma.

I became a regular writer for Microtimes. I re-worked a paper that I had written for a class (about a dead data-via-television technology called VideoText) into another Microtimes article. I had only gotten a B+ on the paper. After it was published, I showed the magazine and the $200 check to the professor. He laughed and said that he would be happy to revisit the grade. But that wasn't necessary — I had $200 and a plan.

※ ※ ※

I graduated in December 1992. Before I went off to college, someone from the university told me there were two undeniable truths: that I would change majors at least once, and that it would take more than four years to graduate. I guess I took that as a personal challenge, because I didn't switch away from the journalism major that I chose at the outset and I managed to finish classes in three and a half years, with two minors — computer information systems and broadcasting.

As for the three-and-a-half-year timeline, I'm not sure what my hurry was. I took as many as 21 units per semester, when as few as 15 were necessary to be considered a full-time student. I took some summer classes too. I am sure that I traded quality of work for speed. My grades weren't great: it's not like I was taking all those classes and pulling straight-As. In the end, it didn't matter: a college diploma is the important thing — no one ever asks to see your grades. Don't tell my daughter, who will be headed for college in a few years, that I wrote that.

The material I learned in the journalism classes served me well. However, a lot of the most useful things that I learned at college had nothing to do with any class; it was stuff that I learned on my own thanks to access to the people, the computer systems, and Internet there. HSU didn't have a single class about the Internet, but by the time I graduated I had spent so much time using and exploring the Internet that I was an expert in tools for Internet users, expertise that I put to use immediately.

Thanks to my pre-graduation running start, I was able to go freelance full-time as soon as I finished school. I pitched editors at every consumer computer magazine that I could find, emphasizing publications that covered the Internet and the online world. This was a unique time where BBSes were still popular, online services like America Online were more popular than ever, and the Internet was just starting to enter the public perception. I wrote for Boardwatch Magazine, a publication devoted to bulletin board systems; Mac Home Journal, a Macintosh magazine; and Online Access, which covered the gamut of BBSes, Internet, and online services.

Those early articles include pieces on the Usenet Oracle, a collaborative humor project which still exists (though it's now called the Internet Oracle), primers on using the Internet, and profiles of early online businesses. I traveled to Colorado to write about ONE BBSCON, a BBS trade show. I wrote about the Project Gutenberg free digital book project, how to use Usenet newsgroups, and Astro-VR, an online service for astronomers. I loved the diversity of subjects that I was able to research and write about. I might not know where my next gig was coming from, but the variety of topics was a plus.

In one of my stranger gigs that first year, I wrote computer tips for a daily fax newsletter. That is, businesses would subscribe to receive this newsletter on their fax machines. Here's my tip for May 24, 1993:

> *ON A WING AND A PRAYER. If you're planning to take your notebook or laptop computer on a trip, know the rules: the FAA recently passed a directive announcing that only "self-contained" computers are allowed — ones with external battery packs, mice, trackballs and so on can't be used. Some airlines have simply banned use of all computers inflight, but others allow self-contained models. Know your airline's policy before you flip that switch.*

I was supposed to be getting $5 a shot for those little blurbs, but after a few months it was hard not to notice that they weren't actually paying for my work. I started calling them, writing letters, and, yes, faxing relentlessly for weeks until finally they paid the invoice just to shut me up.

I also kept on writing for Microtimes — I wrote for them for years, until it faded away in 1998. The number of magazines that I saw come and go in my 14 years of freelancing was boggling. Some were young upstarts — like the glossy Mac magazine that lasted exactly one issue. It was particularly sad and frustrating to see venerable longtime publications such as Byte, which was one of the first computer magazines, go under.

✳ ✳ ✳

Around the time I was finishing college, my PC XT had become beleaguered. It had trouble turning on: I had to flip the big red power switch four or five times before it would acquiesce. Also it was getting loud — the hard drive and fans were tired and noisy. It had a good life, but it was time to let it go. I sold it cheap to a local business owner and suggested that he shouldn't turn it off unless absolutely necessary.

Mom said she'd buy me a new computer. Great — I'd get a Macintosh. I had used Mitch's Mac, and played with the various Macs all around the Humboldt State campus. They were easy to use, they were intuitive, they were fun. But Mom wouldn't buy a Mac; she said PCs were the future. The thought of owning one of those soulless PS/2s didn't excite me at all. So I told her no thanks, then, I'll buy my own Mac. Mom caved and gave me the cash. I bought a Mac IIsi, with a monitor, a 14.4 KBPS modem, and a color inkjet printer. (That IIsi was the first of many Macs that

I have owned. I've also had PCs along the way — as a freelancer, I needed one around for writing Windows software reviews — but for actually getting work done, I'm a Mac guy.)

I signed up for an account on America Online. Now, you might want to laugh at that — but don't. On a practical level, I had few other options for online access: there wasn't a local Internet service provider, and I would soon lose my free ride on the college's Internet connection. Also, that knowledge about AOL ended up being huge for my career down the line. (A couple of years later, I was also a beta-tester for eWorld: Apple's online service which was basically AOL's software, re-branded and with prettier graphics. eWorld was only officially online from 1994 through 1996.)

I joined the local Macintosh users group, comprised of a motley assortment of characters. I became a regular contributor to the group's newsletter, which let me flex my writing chops and was a good source of free (and legal) software. After you reviewed something for the newsletter, you could keep it.

I wrote Macintosh software reviews for many publications, a venture which picked up steam once I invested hundreds of dollars on a 1x SCSI CD-ROM drive. Then I became a regular reviewer for CD-ROM World and Kids & Computers magazines. Some of those discs were terrible — software companies were hot to hop on the CD-ROM bandwagon, and some would shovel anything they could onto the discs just to fill them up. For example: Made in the USA,

an extensive database of information about goods manu-
factured in America; QuickToons, a disc with six "classic"
(read: public domain) cartoons; and Loon Magic, a journey
through the "romance and reality of the world of loons."
Throw some digitized bird photos and sound effects on a
CD, and boom! — a product. Of course, there were some
great discs too. I wrote a review of the groundbreaking
CD-ROM game Myst for Inside Mac Games, a magazine
that was itself published on floppy disk.

※ ※ ※

I primarily focused on consumer- and small business-level
tech subjects. I would accept articles on almost any topic — a
picky freelance writer is a hungry freelance writer. I usually stayed away from anything too "enterprise" oriented:
it was boring.

My first big-name interview was with Steve Case, the
president of America Online, for the January 1994 issue
of Online Access magazine. Titled Shooting For The Star,
it was the magazine's cover article, and it was about AOL
going after Prodigy's spot as the number one online service.
It was one of the few times I had to endure an interview
with "handlers" on the line — a PR person and maybe a
lawyer were listening in on the call, the kind of thing that
never makes an interview subject feel loose and talkative.

Over the years, I interviewed other famous and interesting technology people. In 1993, I interviewed Shuji
Nakamura, the "Thomas Edison of Japan" who invented the

blue laser. His accent was so thick that after I transcribed his quotes, I had to e-mail them to him for clarification and fixes. It turns out I understood almost none of what he had said in our phone interview. In 2005, I interviewed Douglas Engelbart, who invented a lot of the ideas things that we now consider standard on modern computers, including hypertext, word processing, and the graphical user interface. This particular article was devoted to the fact that he invented the mouse. I wish I had a recording of that conversation (but I seldom, if ever, recorded interviews). He was more interested in discussing his philosophy of the future of books, which was interesting but not relevant to the article I needed to deliver. I wish I could have written a general interview article about Englebart — it would have been far more interesting than the few sentences about mice that I was able to coax from him for the piece.

In 1997, I wrote an article about a new online auction site. "The premise of AuctionWeb couldn't be simpler: sell stuff that you don't want, buy stuff that you do want. ... Anyone can put anything up for auction — selling their stuff to the highest bidder as the law of supply and demand runs its course." The URL that I pointed to was www.ebay .com/aw. Eventually, they would drop the AuctionWeb part of the name and just call the site eBay.

My byline appeared in some places that I'm proud to have contributed to, such as Byte, the Washington Post, the International Herald Tribune (ha, they published my article accidentally,) Sesame Street, and Nickelodeon. But for every big-name that I wrote for, I wrote for three little publications that no one ever heard of. Some of those publications quit after just a few issues. Others were sold, merged, mismanaged, or just ran out of time.

I wrote for several magazines that might seem to be a strange fit for me: I was a regular contributor to The Rotarian, even though I'm not a member of Rotary Club. I wrote for Hispanic Business Magazine even though I'm not Hispanic. I wrote for Kids and Computers magazine years before I had a kid, and a United Arab Emirates business magazine even though I couldn't find the UAE on a map. The editors didn't care about those things; they just needed someone who could write about tech and meet the deadlines.

I wrote about cybersex for a glossy Japanese hyper-futurist magazine, and about online photo services for the National Education Association. The job was always changing. Through the variety of topics and publications kept things interesting, making a living as a freelancer would have been impossible without columns — recurring gigs that I could count on month after month. One of my longest-running gigs was for Computer Shopper, from 1999 through 2006, maintaining the listing of top online shopping sites. Every month I went through the list of hundreds of sites, pulling out the companies that had gone out of business and sites that had just gone stale, and replacing them with new listings.

A more painful recurring gig was the BIOS upgrades chart for Computer Power User magazine. Every month I had to pore over a dozen motherboard manufacturers'

Web sites (many of which were not in English) to find out what motherboard firmware upgrades they had released, and create a spreadsheet that listed the data. It usually took two days to gather all of the information. I don't imagine that any reader ever used it.

I learned not to worry when I didn't know anything about the subject of the article assigned to me. I developed a skill, one which many reporters and journalists must have, that I call "writing five minutes behind what I know." That is, I would learn something new (for instance, by interviewing an expert) then five minutes later write about what I'd just learned. I wrote about such diverse subjects as Windows NT (an operating system that I've never used except to write those articles), storage area networks (I'm still not quite sure what those are), customer transaction management systems, and technology-neutral procedures for federated identity management. When I didn't know about a subject, editors trusted me to figure it out and explain it to readers — and in those cases, it *was* easy to explain it to the readers. I could write about the subjects on a basic level because I only had a basic knowledge myself. One time, I tried to not accept an assignment: I told the editor that I didn't understand *anything* about customer relation management systems. He told me "no one understands them" and gave me the job anyway.

Rarely, assignments would take me out into the real world. I co-wrote an occasional feature for Computer Shopper called Rate The Retailers, in which writers from around the country went to various electronics stores to judge the shopping experience. I was the secret shopper at Fry's Electronics, Circuit City, and other stores: I had to find a sales associate and ask questions about a desktop PC that I was allegedly considering. Sometimes the shopping experiences were great, and sometimes they were terrible — with salespeople who were misleading, rude, or pretended I was invisible. (Those experiences, of course, were more fun to write about.)

I also wrote reviews, so many reviews over the years: software, books, hardware. Most of the software I tested, then never touched again. I kept the computer books until my office bookshelves were stuffed full and the towering stacks next to them teetered over.

I liked being among the first to try some new piece of hardware, like an $18,000 enterprise Internet content accelerator appliance, a miniDV camcorder, or the ZIP drive that held 750 MB per disk. It was the hardware roundups that could get tricky. Testing and comparing 20 inkjet printers gets complicated in a tiny home office. There would be printers on the desks and covering every inch of floor space, plus their boxes stacked to the ceiling in the living room downstairs. Another time I wrote reviews of keyboards and mice — there were at least a hundred input devices (plus their boxes, software, and other ephemera) scattered around the house.

When I reviewed an expensive item like a computer or an enterprise Internet content accelerator appliance, the manufacturer always wanted it back when I was done writing. On the other hand, manufacturers very seldom wanted inexpensive items back. It just wasn't worth their time to process it, and what were they going to do with a slightly used printer, mouse, or book, anyway? The publications hardly ever had a policy demanding that I return review units, so I got to quietly keep them. On a small scale, that could be pretty sweet. But it could also be troublesome. What was I supposed to do with 20 inkjet printers? (I kept one for myself and donated the rest to a school.) What was I going to do with scores of keyboards and mice? I gave them away to anyone I knew who wanted a new keyboard and mouse. I kept several for myself. Some of them are still in my basement, ready to be called to action if I have some sort of input device emergency.

INTERNET WORLD

Internet World was one of the earliest magazines about the Internet, and I was one of its early writers. My first articles for that magazine in 1993 covered multi-user dungeons, frequently asked questions and answers lists, and a virtual reality program for astronomers.

The publisher, Mecklermedia, held a trade show in New York which was also called Internet World. I attended a few of them, as a speaker. One talk was about Internet multimedia tools, another was on the basics of using Unix. It was exciting to be flown across the country to speak in front of an audience, but I think I may have been a terrible speaker. I have a recording of one of my talks on cassette tape, but I'm afraid to listen to it. I did my best but ultimately it was a good thing that I do most of my communicating with writing.

On one trip to New York for the Internet World show, I didn't actually make it to the conference. I had flown to NYC alone and took a taxi straight from the airport to a dinner with important people from the show. Once I was seated, I asked the waitress for an iced tea. She walked away without acknowledging my request, so I said — too loudly and rudely — "Or, you could just ignore me." Eventually I got my iced tea and had a nice meal with the important conference people.

I don't know for sure that my rude comment to the waitress was the reason that I got food poisoning a few hours later — that I was the only one from that restaurant who got food poisoning — but there does seem to be a strong correlation between the two events.

After dinner I checked into my room, a tiny space that was the dimmest hotel room ever. In the designers' attempt to create a modern space, they neglected to think about lighting. But that didn't matter much — I was just there to sleep then give my presentation at the conference the next day.

Around midnight, my stomach started feeling not so good. The situation quickly got worse and by the early morning I was crazy sick, with ugly liquid coming from every end, shivering and barely able to stand up. I called down to the front desk and asked for help. They sent someone up to my room to help me walk down to the taxi stand. I asked the taxi driver to take me to the hospital. He refused, he said the hospital was too close, only a few blocks away. New York taxi drivers aren't supposed to do that; they aren't allowed to pick and choose their fares. I wasn't up for an argument, I needed medical assistance. I promised the cabbie a big tip if he just took me to the hospital, please please please. He drove me to the E.R., where I handed him $40 and lurched into the hospital lobby.

A New York City hospital lobby at 3 or 4 in the morning is not a place where people will trust you implicitly. Before the nurses would see me I underwent a gauntlet of passive aggression, paperwork, and a baffling call to my insurance company. Once I was in the E.R., a nurse took one look at me and diagnosed "food poisoning." They gave me some meds and rehydrated me with an IV, and sent me away a couple of hours later. I walked back to the hotel.

Back in my bed, I felt better, but not all better. There was no way I could do my speech at the conference. I called my handler to explain the situation, then spent the rest of my time in New York City lying in bed in my dim, dim room. The Mecklermedia folks were kind and gracious about the whole thing, and paid my expenses as promised even though all I did for them in New York was eat their food then throw it up again.

The next year I was invited back to that conference, and things went better. I gave my presentation the first morning, then decided to leave the convention center and just walk around. I walked and walked, covering every inch of Times Square and Rockefeller Center. The next day I walked some more; I had a great time just exploring Manhattan by myself.

The next time I was back, a year or two later, I realized that I just knew where things were. I am usually a person with a terrible sense of direction. I thank the gods at Garmin every day for GPS; otherwise I'd get lost each time I drive a car. But when walking around Manhattan, I know how to get around. Just two long days of strolling around somehow imbibed me with a sense of direction, which only works in one part of a city 2,500 miles from where I live.

A year or two later, Peace and I went to another Internet World conference, this time in Boston, where I did a book signing on the show floor. After the show, we went to a party at the home of Robert Metcalfe, founder of 3Com and inventor of Ethernet. He had a beautiful house complete with a big-screen media room that impressed me like crazy. It was a bizarre thing, to be at Bob's house and shaking his hand. Maybe we were young and easily impressed, but it felt like the equivalent of being invited to a fancy party at Thomas Edison's place. "Hi, I'm Tom, I invented the lightbulb. Wanna see my media room?" (I guess Tom's media room would have been a zoetrope or something, but that would have been bizarre and awesome too.)

SEQUOIA TECHNICAL SERVICES

I had a job in an office for a few years, simultaneously with the freelance writing. It was, now that I think about it, the only drive-to-an-office, work-with-others job that I've ever had. Getting a job after college was what you were supposed to do, so I dutifully did. Peace and I wanted regular paychecks to keep the rent paid; freelance writing seemed too uncertain. So I'm jumping back to mid-1993 for the "Meanwhile, back at the ranch ..." portion of the story.

In June 1993, I was hired by a little company in Eureka, California called Sequoia Technical Services. The company's main mission was helping people choose energy-efficient lighting and windows, but I was hired because the owner, Larry, had a vision to create a community bulletin board system to help bring together the rural communities of Northern California. I was to design the system, then be the system operator.

From the November 1993 issue of the local Macintosh users group newsletter:

> *The Northcoast Electronic Town (NET) will link the citizens, businesses and government of five Northern California counties ... Using four 14.4 modems, the system will offer nearly 2 gigabytes of information (including two CD ROM disks with Mac and Windows software) and a 24-hour help line for technical assistance to support the system.*

Larry invested more than $20,000 in the project. I drove to the FedEx facility to pick up the Mac Quadra computer, then stayed late at the office setting it up. The system used FirstClass BBS software: users could send e-mail, participate in message boards, and learn about community events. Access to the NET cost $10 a month for two hours online, then $5 an hour for additional time. Larry's idea to use a bulletin board system for general community information and dialogue was a good one, but the timing wasn't right — BBSes were on the way out; the Internet was coming.

Nevertheless, I spent countless hours setting up and maintaining the Northcoast Electronic Town. There was a fax server, so users could send faxes from the BBS; a Usenet gateway that never worked reliably; and best of all, Peace's voice welcoming you every time you logged in.

The first time I used the World Wide Web was in those offices. I don't remember if we had a high-speed (128kbps) connection at that point or if I was using dial-up. But I do remember using FTP to download the Web browser, NCSA Mosaic, and running the program. The experience was awful. Downloading those graphics felt so slow, and the browser crashed constantly. I tried "surfing the Web" for maybe 10 minutes and then gave up, annoyed.

There was no way that slow, crashy Web would become more popular than Gopher. Gopher was a text-based, menu-based system for browsing information. Because it was all text, it was fast. When you started the Gopher client software, you always started in the same place — Gopher's main menu at the University of Minnesota (where it was developed). The menus imposed a strong hierarchy on information — you could choose Libraries or News or Phone Books, for instance — making the information you wanted easy to find.

The Web, on the other hand, had no main menu — you could set your homepage to be anywhere. And there was no listing of everything on the Web, so how were you supposed to find anything? I was unimpressed by my first experience with the Web, but it quickly got better.

Ha! I just did a Google search to get a screenshot of the main Gopher menu at UMN, and was surprised to find, on page 1 of the search results, the screenshot from my own Web site. Here's what Gopher looked like:

```
Gopher headquarters (gopher.tc.umn.edu)

     1.  Information About Gopher/
     2.  Computer Information/
     3.  Discussion Groups/
     4.  Fun & Games/
     5.  Internet file server (ftp) sites/
     6.  Libraries/
 ->  7.  News/
     8.  Other Gopher and Information Servers/
     9.  Phone Books/
    10.  Search Gopher Titles at the University
         of Minnesota <?>
    11.  Search lots of places at the University
         of Minnesota  <?>
    12.  University of Minnesota Campus
         Information/
```

In 1994, a year or so after building the Northcoast Electronic Town, the company became the first Internet service provider (ISP) in Humboldt County. The only options for an Internet connection in the area at that time were the university (which was useless if you weren't a student or faculty member) and America Online (which was pretty much useless for Internet no matter who you were). I had nagged Larry about it for months — the area needed a real ISP, and we were the people who could make it happen.

Larry took a huge risk and put up a lot of money to create Northcoast Internet. It took four people to build the ISP: Larry was the business guy, I was the system administrator, Fred was network administrator, and Rhonda answered the phones and the mail. Rhonda thought we were all crazy.

Northcoast Internet was a hit. People wanted Internet access, badly. On the night that we launched the service with a public unveiling in the ballroom of the Red Lion hotel, we garnered a couple hundred subscribers. After the launch event, and after we unloaded all of our gear back into the office, I stayed late and entered all the new subscribers' accounts into the terminal server by hand. The modems were lighting up with users even before I turned off the lights and locked up. The service launched with fourteen 14.4kbps modems and a 128kbps frame relay connection for the Internet connectivity.

Larry dropped big bucks on a Sparc workstation that would be our first Web server, Usenet server, and everything else server. I learned a lot as system administrator, created install disks, wrote documentation, and tried to keep users from doing stupid things. Sometimes I could only try to clean up the mess after users did stupid things. One weekend a subscriber, a local business owner, was feeling horny and posted an explicit message on Usenet, asking for (women? men? whatever he was into) to call him — on his company's toll-free phone number. The calls came — and kept coming, and were still coming Monday morning when his employees came to work to answer the phones. He called us in a panic, asking us to stop the calls from coming. You can "kill" a message on Usenet, which should have made his message invisible, but he couldn't figure out how to do it. I tried to help, but I was unable to properly forge a kill message using my computer ... so he had to endure a humiliating and expensive lesson in using the Internet.

I worked for Sequoia Technical/Northcoast Internet for a few years, always continuing to write on the side, but the writing was where my heart was, so after a while I bowed out.

BACK TO BLUE LAKE

Peace and I married in July 1994. We were living in a two-bedroom apartment in Arcata, not far from the college, but we wanted to get a house. Around that time Mitch's family was getting ready to sell their house in Blue Lake, so Peace and I bought the house from them. It was a great solution — I had already lived in the house, so I knew exactly what its problems were. Also, buying from friends let us skip some of the annoyances that can go along with buying a house. For one thing, neither party used a real estate agent; instead we filed the paperwork ourselves. Peace and I moved in on Christmas Eve 1994. The little attic room — originally Mitch's great-grandma's sewing room, then The Bridge — was re-christened again, becoming my home office. Owning it meant we could paint it something other than pink.

The house needed some updating. One of the first things we did was call an electrician to add grounded electrical plugs to the office — the computers would like that better. I hired a kitchen cabinet guy to create built-in desks and bookshelves that worked around the office's low sloped ceiling, and I was back in business.

The little city of Blue Lake had a population of about 1,200 people. It was often sunny, usually quiet, and a beautiful place to live. You could walk to the Mad River or watch the cows grazing in their fields. There was no home mail delivery — every day we'd walk to the post office to get the mail. It was quaint, but by this time, the phone company had added Touch-Tone dialing, so it's not like we were living in the Dark Ages.

CHAPTER 10
FAQS AND BOOKS

So in 1994 I was working as a freelance writer and working at Sequoia Technical Services. I still managed to have free time (because my daughter wasn't born until 1997) and I spent some of that time on Usenet, primarily in a newsgroup called alt.internet.services.

Alt.internet.services was the place for talking about Internet tools and services. A common problem on newsgroups was that different people would tend to post the same basic questions again and again. The regular posters want to help answer the newbies' questions, but it gets to be a drag answering the same old basic queries again and again. The solution is something called a FAQ, or frequently asked questions and answers list. With a FAQ, someone collects the common questions, along with really good, definitive answers to each, into a document that gets posted to the newsgroup on a regular basis. The newbies can read the FAQ instead of posting their basic questions for the millionth time.

I had time on my hands, wanted to help, and knew a lot of the answers, so I stepped up and wrote the alt. internet.services FAQ list. It answered questions like: I'm new to the Internet. Where do I start? Why isn't there an encyclopedia on the Internet? How do I send mail from the Internet to another network? How do I find out someone's e-mail address?

That FAQ document seemed to be popular and helpful, so I created some others. One of the common questions in the alt.internet.services FAQ was about how to send a fax from the Internet. The answer started to get complicated and unwieldy, so in April 1994 I created a new FAQ document that just answered the question: "How can I send a fax from the Internet?" It listed a grand total of four Internet fax services, one of which was a service that would only send faxes to Russia. I also created "The Unofficial Internet Book List," which was a list of books about the Internet. At the time, it was possible to maintain a fairly complete list of Internet-related books — there just weren't that many out there yet.

A few months later I created another FAQ document: "How can I use the Internet as a telephone?" and, along with a collaborator, a document called "Internet Press: A Guide to Electronic Journals About the Internet."

I had become the FAQ man for that little corner of the Internet. My goals were to help people who needed information about using the Internet, and also to keep myself up-to-date about the technology. At the time, there was a real sense of "giving back to the Net," of helping others in the community. So I created those FAQ files to help others, but karmically that volunteer work ending up benefiting me. The Internet Services FAQ led to my first book, which was essentially a very, very expanded Q&A about the Internet.

The fax FAQ has remained popular. I still maintain it, though I moved it from Usenet to the Web a long time ago. It's at www.savetz.com/fax and today it lists a whole lot more than four faxing services. It amazes me that a document that I started writing on a whim in 1994 could still remain relevant and useful 18 years later. I tried to stop updating the fax FAQ for a while, but it just wouldn't die. It remained at the top spot in Google despite months of neglect, and I kept getting e-mails from all over the world with questions about faxing. Finally I had to throw up my hands in defeat and started updating the material again — that document I had created when I was 22 just refused to go away. In 2005, I launched a separate site, FaxAnswers .com, to answer other questions about faxing. I just might be the fax answer guy forever, or until people finally stop using fax machines. Which, since that hasn't happened yet, might never happen.

My other FAQs were easier to let go when the time came. Most just weren't necessary anymore after a time. I maintained the Unofficial Internet Book List until 1997. At that point, the list had 884 books in it, and was a half megabyte in size. Many publishers were sending me piles of new books as they were released: books about ActiveX and virtual reality markup language and other cutting-edge Internet tech were piled high. Publishers were starting to figure out that the Internet was a real thing, speeding up production of new books, so keeping that list updated became a Sisyphean task. When people became aware of Amazon and other online bookstores that not only had a listing of books, but let you buy them, my list had become redundant, so I stopped updating it.

BOOKS

Your Internet Consultant: The FAQs of Life Online was the title of my first book. I used my alt.internet.services FAQ as a jumping-off point — the book was a 600-page Q&A-fest about the Internet. I had contributed to a couple of other projects for that publisher: thick, multi-author tomes called Internet Unleashed and Tricks of the Internet Gurus, and had proven myself capable enough to write a book on my own. It was a tough job, but so gratifying to have that finished book in hand at the end. Your Internet Consultant hit a couple of best-seller lists for a microsecond, and was translated into a few other languages.

One of my earliest contributions to a book was a ghost-writing gig, and it was a rush job. The publisher had come to the conclusion that the writer wasn't going to get the job done by deadline, so contracted me to write 100 pages in under three weeks. They'd pay $5,000 for churning out 30,000 words about downloading pictures from the Internet. I worked day and night, and got the job done. The job was satisfying — but not getting my name on the cover was not.

Online, in tune

Arcata author publishes book that answers Internet's greatest mysteries

By Devanie Anderson
For The Union

'The Internet, like any society, has its own culture, and I found it fun to go into that a little bit.'
— Kevin Savetz

Kevin Savetz, 23, wrote "Your Internet Consultant — The FAQs of Life Online," which covers topics from bulletin board systems to games to E-mail to information storehouses.

Devanie Anderson/The Union

My friend Devanie wrote an article about me and my first book for the Arcata Union newspaper, published August 18, 1994. Best quote: "The former Atari player expects to be around to see a computer society in which the Internet is as common as cable television."

I tried to write a couple of books on cutting-edge technologies, in an attempt to have the first book in the bookstores when the next big technology hit. That led to co-writing MBONE: Multicasting Tomorrow's Internet, which was published by IDG in April 1996. The MBONE, or Multicast Backbone, was supposed to deliver thousands of channels of multimedia content on the Internet by sending each in one stream that users could tap into. (At least, I think so. I don't remember anymore, and I'm not sure I ever fully understood it.) The MBONE never caught on;

streaming technologies like RealMedia delivered multimedia without its complexity.

My other cutting-edge book experiment was a user's guide to BeOS for O'Reilly and Associates. BeOS was a hot new forward-thinking operating system that didn't widely catch on before the company imploded. My co-author and I had written about half of the book before the publisher saw the writing on the wall and cancelled the project. Because of that project, I did end up with a BeBox, a semi-rare dual-processor computer which now lives in my basement. I like that BeOS fans have kept its spirit alive with Haiku, an open-source operating system that remains compatible with BeOS source code and binaries. (www.haiku-os.org)

I had another book project that just couldn't get off the ground. "Internet Top Ten Lists" was going to be published by Sybex in 1994, as a humorous book of lists about the Internet. The lists would include "E-mail addresses of ten famous people" (like Ross Perot and Billy Idol) and "Four facts about libraries on the 'net." (Here's one: the Seattle Public Library was the first in the United States to provide free public computer terminals for Internet access.)

When I was about three-quarters done writing, Sybex cancelled the project "due to marketing considerations." I shopped the idea around, and in 1995, O'Reilly and Associates agreed to use the lists in Internet User Tools, which was going to be a group-written book about Internet clients. That book was never published either. By that time, some of the top ten lists were getting stale and I was tired of the project, so the book never saw the light of day. I was happy, though, having been paid partial advances on an unfinished book from two different publishers. A decade later, I put the 158 unpublished lists on up on my Web site. (www.savetz.com/topten/)

Here's one of the lists, which is probably thrilled to make it into an actual book after almost 20 years. (None of these resources work anymore; don't bother trying.)

Top five funkiest things ever hooked to the net

1. The legendary Internet Toaster

In 1990, a wily hacker named John Romkey hooked his Sunbeam Deluxe Automatic Radiant Control Toaster to the Internet. You could only control one thing — the power — via the 'net. When the power went off, it automatically popped the toast.

2. Cola machines at various colleges

Why not? Students at colleges around the United States have hooked cola machines to the 'net so they can check the inventory right from the computer lab. Why walk all the way down the hall just to discover the machine is out of Jolt? (finger drink@drink.csh. rit.edu, finger pony@sail.stanford.edu, finger coke@cs.cmu.edu)

3. A hot tub

Don't ask me why he did so, but this guy hooked his hot tub to a computer on the 'net — you can check the water temperature, the temperature of the outside air and other pertinent hot tub information. No, I didn't say this was useful. (finger hottub@ hamjudo.com or e-mail hottub@hamjudo.com).

Here's an example of what it looks like when you finger Paul's hot tub. Wish I was there.
$ finger hottub@hamjudo.com
Paul's hottub is a bit warm at about 102 degrees Fahrenheit.
It is nice outside at about 71 degrees Fahrenheit.
The ozone generator is working. The cover is closed.
The backup battery is OK at 10.3 volts (this will still work down to 6 volts)

4. A coffee pot
Will that be regular or decaf today? If you use Mosaic (or another graphical Web browser) you can peer at a coffee pot in a corner of the "Trojan Room" at Cambridge University. Thanks to a video frame grabber that takes a picture of the coffee pot once a second, users at Cambridge (or anywhere else) can find out if there's any coffee available. (www.cl.cam.ac.uk)

5. A thermometer in an office somewhere in Maine
In another example of useless tomfoolery, a gentleman named Andrew Sheaff has connected his office thermometer to the Internet. By telneting to a certain address, you can check the temperature. Too bad you can't turn his heat up, too! (telnet small.eece.maine.edu 9876)

Another silly book project, which actually was published, was called net.sex. I co-wrote this book with two friends. The three of us wrote it pseudonymously, under the names Candi Rose and Dirk Thomas. Sams published it in December 1994. We were annoyed at the time that Ziff Davis simultaneously published a book also called Net.Sex, but the book sold pretty well nonetheless.

We went out of our way to keep the book rated PG. Our proposal emphasized the fact that it would be smut-free. "Notice in this outline that we aren't planning a glossy fold-out section of our favorite girlie pictures ... Although the book is intended for adults, we intend to treat the readers like adults without pandering to the lowest common denominator."

Library Journal's review of the book said: "Let's start off by saying this contains no pictures except for six photos of a Himalayan peak as a way to explain picture formats (really!) ... Both authors obviously enjoy exploring the possibilities of cyberintimacy, and it shows in their writing. The first half takes readers on a quick visit to different lists and Usenet groups, from the most mundane to the outrageous. The second half treats Internet Relay Chat and MUDs as well as ways to download files. ... The real value of this book, however, comes in a snapshot of the current state of online encounters. As an anthropological or psychological document, or as an enlightened introduction, you'll find net.sex a guide to thinking about sex in an entirely different way."

Wow, Library Journal was generous in its opinion of our little book, which we knocked out in a month so or because we thought it would be fun and easy.

I co-wrote a couple of other books, including one about America Online. For the Official America Online Internet Guide: Macintosh Version (not a title that just rolls off the tongue), I took the Windows edition of the Official America Online Internet Guide and rewrote it for the Macintosh audience. I recall taking lots and lots of screenshots, and cutting entire swaths of the Windows version out because the Mac version of AOL lacked many of the features in the Windows version.

Eventually I made the choice to stay away from books, instead sticking to magazine and newspaper articles. Whether I measured it per-word or on a time-spent basis, articles paid better than books. Also, I got bored writing about the same topic for a book-length project — it was more stimulating to cover two, three, or four different technical subjects in a week.

Sooner or later, often sooner, computer books go out of print. I always tried to get a clause in my contract with the publisher that when a book did go out of print, the rights would revert to me. I made Your Internet Consultant and the MBONE book available at my personal Web site soon after the publishers were done with them. As long as I had the information, I figured why not make it available for free on the Web where it might benefit someone? (When Google AdSense came along, I put ads on the book Web pages. Over the years, I think I've earned more from the ads on the Your Internet Consultant Web site (www.savetz.com/yic/) than I earned from the printed version. Then again, it wasn't a hard number to beat. The publisher wasn't too generous.)

The content of that book was pretty fantastic when the book was published in 1994 (if I do say so myself) and was probably still useful when I first made it available on the Web. Then it just got old. Now, it's kind of an interesting glimpse into the way the Internet used to be, with its chapters about Usenet and FTP and pedantic discussion about "netiquette." Today it can practically be used as a historical document, but you wouldn't want to try to learn about the modern Internet from it. Which is why I laughed and laughed when I received an e-mail in 2012, from a person who apparently discovered the online version of Your Internet Consultant for the first time and didn't understand its age or purpose. The letter, written by fellow who identified himself only as Dick, was filled with venom and nasty language. Dick took umbrage because I said that the Internet is hard to learn to use ("it might be for &^@!s like you," he wrote), that it "is almost completely disorganized," and that "there is too much information on the Internet." It's surprising to me that a few Web pages with an old book about the Internet would elicit such contempt.

Yes, the Internet has changed dramatically since I wrote that book, mostly for the better. The Internet *was* hard to learn to use. At its core, it's probably as disorganized as it ever was, but search engines sure do bring a semblance of structure to things. I agree with my new friend Dick, however: there can never be too much information on the Net.

CHAPTER 11
ANSWERMAN AND MICROSOFT BOOKSHELF

David, my editor at Sybex, had switched jobs: now he was at America Online. David called me up and asked if I wanted to run an Internet help forum on AOL. The forum would be called Internet AnswerMan, and I would be its namesake.

He sent me some concept art for the AnswerMan forum: it showed a happy fat man in a fez who was smoking a pipe. I have no idea what might have been in the pipe that the artist was smoking, but the contracts were signed and before long I was in charge of the de facto Internet help center on America Online. The forum opened in December 1995.

At the time, AOL subscribers paid $9.95 for up to five hours of online time, then $3.95 per hour for additional time. AOL offered to give me a small cut of the income from every hour users spent in my forum. Well, 39.5 cents an hour doesn't seem like a lot, but I owned the Internet help forum. It was 1996. People wanted the Internet, bad. And people needed Internet help. Those AOL users logged thousands of hours every month in my forum.

There were other Internet-related areas on AOL, including the NetGirl forum and the In Business forum, for early adopters who wanted to do business on the Internet in 1995. When I started, AOL's Internet offerings were limited to e-mail, FTP, and Gopher. During my tenure, they added a Web browser, the holy grail of Internet access.

I shredded the tax records long ago in a fit of cleaning, so I can't tell you exactly how much the AnswerMan forum earned me, but it was big money every month. Peace and I built an addition onto our house — a master bedroom and bathroom, and re-did the kitchen — paying cash for it all.

All I had to do was write a newsletter once a week, host occasional live online chats, and answer some questions in the messages bases about how to use the Internet. I did it all from my little attic office at home. It was a dream gig.

America Online users have a reputation for being clueless newbies, and I suppose that some of them were — but it's not fair to judge someone for wanting to learn something new. Most of the users that I dealt with were kind and smart, although sometimes frustrated with learning the complexities of the Internet on AOL's not-always-intuitive system. One woman, however, railed against the AnswerMan forum

The AnswerMan forum.

Draft art for AnswerMan featuring him in a **fez** and pipe, the proper attire for using the Internet.

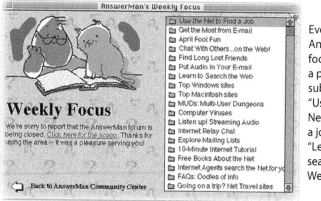

Every week AnswerMan focused on a particular subject like: "Use the Net to find a job" and "Learn to search the Web."

because she said the name was sexist. I didn't know how to answer that charge — I'm the person with the answers, and I'm a man, how is that sexist?

After several months, AOL wanted to add another Internet help area to the service, at keyword: INTERNET HELP. This would be a more centralized help area, with official answers rather than a newsletter and forum. They wanted me to help write it, but for Internet Help, AOL was only willing to pay half of the per-user-per-hour rate that they paid for AnswerMan. I jumped at the chance — even at half the hourly rate, it could easily get double the hours of AnswerMan. Plus, I'd still be running AnswerMan. The work was grueling: there were tons of common questions about the Internet to answer before the Internet Help forum could open. When it did, the effort paid off.

Here's a particularly painful little taste. We had to spell out every little thing because "surfing" the "Web" was so new to everyone.

The AOL 3.0 for Windows95 software uses Microsoft's Internet Explorer as its built-in Web browser. This enables you to use the most up to date features of the WWW while browsing from America Online.

Many of the newest features are built in to the software, but there are occasions where you will want to adjust your preferences. The browser preferences can be reached by clicking the Prefs button on the browser window itself, or by choosing Preferences, then WWW, from your Members menu at the top of the screen. ...

The Navigation section has a few ways to make your "surfing" easier, by allowing you to change your start page, remember your favorite search sites, and set up "Quicklinks" that you can jump to at any time. Below this portion, you have your stored History, which remembers every site you visit. Boxes here allow you to set the number of days that sites are stored, as well as a place to View all of your History, or clear it and start over.

AOL gave me a couple of free accounts, and I gave one of them to my mom. I told her to have fun online but recommended that she stay out of the chat rooms because they were filled with weirdos. I'll give you just one guess where she met her future husband.

Here's a story George, the future husband, told me. He had told a friend that he was dating a woman that he met online. In the course of the conversation he mentioned that the woman's son worked for AOL. "Oh? What does he

AOL's Net Help area.

do?" — "He is the Internet AnswerMan." — "You're dating AnswerMan's mom!?!"

In November 1996, AOL announced that it would switch to a flat-rate pricing plan: $19.95 a month for all-you-can-eat service. I wondered how they would handle paying content providers like me: without charging an hourly rate, they couldn't afford to pay a few cents for every hour that people spent online. In May 1997, my handlers at AOL offered me a new deal: a flat monthly fee that was far, far less than I had been earning under the old system. I was trying to decide what to do. Then, in an abrupt mood shift a few days later, they decided to simply shut down the AnswerMan forum. They pulled the plug on AnswerMan, and suddenly that gig was done. The 70,000 subscribers to my newsletter seemed baffled. I took my fez and went home.

While writing this, I found on the Web a memorial to AnswerMan created by someone named David Frisk. I don't know David. It has that flavor of a Web site that was created with loving care in 1997, then virtually ignored for 15 years. (doorsclosing.com/lursk/answerman/) David saved all the AnswerMan newsletters and chat transcripts that he could, plus some of the graphics from the forum. He also wrote a wonderful little eulogy. Here's a bit of it:

> *Who was AnswerMan? Well, that's not a difficult question in itself. AnswerMan is who he always has been — Kevin Savetz, sometimes freelance writer and Internet user. He's not famous, or well known, but he has written a few things that people bought (which is more than you can say for most of the Internet). But in the middle of the 90's, Kevin Savetz was more than just a freelancer. He was a force to be reckoned with on the AOL servers.*

> *Achieving quite a bit of popularity, The AnswerMan was more than just a figurehead to the company that employed him, America Online. While he may have been forced to play by their rules, he did something that most did not — and never have — associated with the company. He was nice.*

> *Must be why he was fired.*

I wanted to continue helping people learn about the Internet, and they wanted me. In my final newsletter, which I sent out without AOL's authorization, I did something drastic: I explained that AOL was shutting AnswerMan down, but announced that I was starting my own newsletter, called "Internet Extra," and invited people to subscribe by sending a check — $12 for 52 weekly issues.

The powers that be at AOL were pissed. They were probably pissed that I had outed their capriciousness as the reason the forum was being closed, and they were definitely pissed that I was hitting their customers up for my own venture. They couldn't do anything about the thousands of newsletters that had already been e-mailed, but they redacted the online version by removing my farewell to the community and the information about my new newsletter.

I had exactly one chance to get some of those 70,000 readers to subscribe to my newsletter. PayPal (or any sort of safe online payment system) was still years away, so people needed to send a check. I received maybe 100 checks in the mail. After publishing a couple of newsletters, it was clear no more checks would come in, I knew that my independently published newsletter wouldn't be profitable. With more chances to reach AnswerMan's former audience I might have been able to make my first venture as an online publisher work. I returned the money.

In retrospect, I know that what I did was wrong, even if AOL was making stupid decisions. Surprisingly, my final newsletter didn't burn bridges at AOL. In later years I did some freelance writing for them, including writing marketing and technical copy for You've Got Pictures, a digital film developing tool; and AOL's HomeTown Web site publishing tool. Not surprisingly, AOL still hasn't learned not to unplug useful things that its customers liked. In 2008, AOL shut down HomeTown, despite the fact that it was still home to more than 14 million Web sites that its users had created.

AOL wasn't my only run-in with providing content for an online service. In 1997, I got a gig writing a newsletter for an Internet forum on CompuServe. I called the newsletter Internet Extra (sound familiar?) and wrote it every week. Well, I was supposed to write it weekly but the forum people were flexible when I fell behind. Later, I became freelance staff for a new CompuServe forum devoted to Internet multimedia. Discussion areas in that forum included streaming media, Internet telephony and videoconferencing, and "Life at 56 KBPS and up." The forum didn't catch on like AnswerMan did, for many reasons. For one, there were many Internet-related forums competing for users' attention on CompuServe. For my part, I wasn't too invested in making that forum work: it wasn't making big money and my attention was divided with other projects.

Naturally that gig included an account on CompuServe that cost nothing. I never used that account except for the minimum needed to do my newsletter and forum work. Just a few years before I would have done anything for a free CompuServe account, but by now it was turning into an anachronism — it was a text-based service while America Online and other services were pretty graphical worlds, and it was a private, walled garden that was isolated from the open, free Internet.

MICROSOFT BOOKSHELF

In 1994, Daniel Dern, who was my editor at Internet World magazine, e-mailed and told me he had been offered a huge project for Microsoft which he had no interest in doing — because it sounded like a terrible amount of work and endless amounts of pain. Instead, he recommended to Microsoft that I was the guy for the job.

The project was to create a Web directory for Microsoft Bookshelf. Bookshelf was a CD-ROM which contained several reference books, including an encyclopedia, thesaurus, almanac, and so on. Microsoft wanted to add a directory of the best Web sites. Decent search engines killed the Web directory business, but for a while every publisher was creating giant phone books with lists of Web sites — one popular title was actually called The Internet Yellow Pages. You'd look up the subject that you were interested in, like cars or philosophy, then browse descriptions of the best Web sites on those subjects.

So for Bookshelf 95, Microsoft wanted to create a directory of 5,000 Web sites. It sounded like a terrible amount of work and endless amounts of pain. I took the gig.

I needed to hire a stable of writers — 5,000 entries was way too much for one person to research and write. My plan was to do some of the writing myself, but primarily to serve as an editor, doling out category assignments to the writers, then proofreading their work before handing it off to Microsoft.

Those writers would need to be paid. Microsoft preferred to deal with just one vendor (me) and let me pay the writers as subcontractors. Our contract said that they'd start by paying 50 percent of the project price in advance, a big chunk of which I'd use to pay the writers. They sent the check, so I drove to the bank to open a business checking account and deposit it. Until that point as a freelance writer, I had been using my personal bank account as the business account too. Now seemed like the time to act like a real business and get a separate bank account.

So I walked into our bank in Arcata. As I've probably made clear already, Arcata is a little college town nestled between giant redwood trees and the foggy Pacific coast. It isn't exactly Manhattan. At the time, the city had a population of about 16,000, and a median family income of $36,000. I walked into the bank dressed like I always dress — jeans, t-shirt, and sandals. My shirt that day was tie-dyed and featured Arlo Guthrie on an easy chair floating in space. I did not look the part of serious professional businessman.

I walked up to the teller for business accounts, who glanced up at me for a microsecond before looking back down to her work. She slowly finished her project before looking up at me with a measure of apathy. I said that I wanted to open a business account, and it seemed like she couldn't have cared less — she would get the paperwork for me but only when she was good and ready. When she asked what my opening deposit would be, I slid the check from Microsoft across her desk — for $64,500. Her attitude changed in an instant — suddenly I was Mr. Savetz, and she was all smiles. "Yes, Mr. Savetz," "Just one moment, Mr. Savetz." She was obsequiousness personified. A minute later, the bank manager had taken over. I didn't have any more trouble getting my new account set up.

I hired 15 or so writers, some of whom I already knew and some whom I didn't. I had never hired staff before and did a terrible job. A few of the writers were fantastic, professionals who wrote polished prose. A handful were terrible, producing copy that was barely intelligible. And since those people were incapable of writing, they were incapable of re-writing. Luckily, I'd married Peace by this time and she knew how to read and write. Peace and I ended up throwing away a lot of their work and writing entire categories of Web site descriptions from scratch. It was exhausting. Peace still complains about having to rewrite the entire automotive section after it was bungled. Then and now she has zero interest in cars. She didn't even have a driver's license until she was 23.

I would need a fast Internet connection to make this project possible. I had dial-up with the fastest modem you could get — 28.8kbits per second. Cable Internet access wasn't available in Blue Lake yet, nor was DSL. (In fact, the last time I checked, DSL still wasn't available there. I think the phone company is still pleased with itself for upgrading the switch to handle Touch-Tone.) The phone company did offer ISDN service. However, there wasn't an ISP anywhere in the county that offered an ISDN connection. If I got ISDN, I would have to dial long distance to the nearest ISDN ISP, in Santa Cruz. Also, I'd need new hardware — an ISDN router and Ethernet equipment. My handlers at Microsoft asked for a shopping list, and the next week I received a box with all the hardware I needed. When both channels of the ISDN connection were active, I had 112 kbits per second at my disposal. It was so much speeder than dial-up and allowed both Peace and I to work online at the same time. By the time the project was finished a few months later, we had racked up a long-distance bill of more than $1,200. Microsoft didn't bat an eyelash; they just paid the bill. Microsoft clearly knew how to throw money at a problem.

A few weeks into the project, the folks from Microsoft seemed worried about how things were going, so my manager announced that they were going to fly three people down from Redmond, Washington to my office for a meeting. It was so intimidating — three people from Microsoft coming down to my little office in the attic of my house in a town of 1,200. And now, on top of doing this massive project (and making it look like there was significant progress before they arrived) we had to clean the house!

The three people turned out to be very nice, and they brought armloads of software — every Microsoft product that I said that I needed (which included the just-released Windows 95 and the latest version of Flight Simulator). The meeting was stressful, and boiled down to: "Get the damn book written." After the meeting, the Microsoft people, my wife and I went to the beach. It was surreal.

In the end, the Microsoft Bookshelf Internet Directory ended up with about 4,500 entries — short of the 5,000 that I had promised to Microsoft, but I think they were happy enough with the work. In addition to the Bookshelf CD-ROM, they published the directory as a thick book.

A footnote to the story: Microsoft wanted to add to the Internet Directory for the 1996 edition of Bookshelf, but this time they decided to do the editorial work in-house. Which was fine with us — Peace and I didn't want to go through that project again. However, the company still preferred to pay a single vendor rather than a dozen different writers, so they were going to pay the writers through an a employment service. On a whim, I said, "I'll be your employment service for half of whatever fee they'd charge you." I said that having absolutely no idea what work was involved in being an employment service, or what kind of fee an employment service even charged. Microsoft agreed to my terms. It turns out the work that was involved was simply writing a few checks and sending out tax forms. For that meager work, Microsoft paid me a 12.5% premium over whatever they were paying their writers. They paid me thousands of dollars to write some checks. It almost made up for the terrible amount of work and endless amounts of pain the first time around.

MAGAZINE EDITOR

I'm keeping the specifics of this story vague. I don't want go get sued.

In 2002, I got an interesting offer to be the editor of a new computer magazine for New York City. The pay was a gamble — a percentage of the magazine's profits — but I liked the idea of being an editor and thought that it could lead to more lucrative editing jobs later. The publisher gave me a small budget for writers, so I hired some of my freelance friends and put together the first issue of the magazine. I made assignments, edited the articles, wrote headlines, and packaged it all up for layout. A stack of the magazines arrived in my mailbox and they looked pretty good. It was a thrill to have my name at the top of the masthead for a change, instead of way down at the bottom as a contributor. I was proud of the work. I got to work on issue two, e-mailed the publisher with some questions, and didn't get a response. I e-mailed him again a few days later, then tried calling. Nothing. I never heard from that man again.

Business ventures fail. Magazines sometimes fail to attract advertisers and have to be scrapped early on. It happens all the time; there's no shame in it. The shameful part comes when your magazine fails and you don't even bother to e-mail the editor who worked on the project for weeks (for free).

In the end, the project earned me the ability to say I had been a magazine editor, and (for some reason) a handful of pens and a t-shirt with the logo from a Sci-Fi channel miniseries, ironically titled "Taken."

CHAPTER 12
WEB SITES

I created my first personal Web site in October 1994. I registered my first domain name, savetz.com, on December 5, less than a month before Peace and I bought our house in Blue Lake. I coded the HTML by hand, with a text editor. (I don't think there was a choice; there weren't any good HTML editors yet.) That's a skill that's served me well over the years: I still do HTML coding by hand.

I'm happy with the choices I've made in life and don't believe in wasting emotional energy on regrets. What's done is done. But it's hard not to think about the missed opportunity back then in registering domain names. If I had registered toys.com, cars.com, realestate.com or any of a thousand other generic noun domain names which were all available then, I would be a kabillionaire today. Peace and some friends had talked about doing it, but I didn't seriously consider gambling on buying random domain names. They were expensive — a buyer needed to plunk down $70 for the first two years — and we didn't have much extra money.

I did have extra time, and I used some of it to create silly pages on that site which became popular. I had a set of bath toys: they were foam, shaped like fish, and each fish had a number on it. I used the flatbed scanner in the Northcoast Internet office to scan the foam fish, then wrote a Perl script to display the time using the pictures of the fish. "Foam Bath Fish Time" was a huge hit. (www.savetz .com/fishtime/fishtime.cgi)

I made this Web page just for the halibut.

In September 1995, I created a page called Kevin's Fridge Magnets. Back at the flatbed scanner, I scanned a set of refrigerator magnets and wrote a Perl script that spelled out whatever you typed in magnets. It was crazy popular, and mentioned in many books and magazine articles about the Internet. I know why it was popular back then: the concept was novel, and it was interesting to see your message shown back to you in the form of magnets. What I don't understand is why the page is still used today (at www.savetz.com/fridge/fridge.cgi) when there are so many more interesting things to do on the Web. I wouldn't call it "popular" anymore, but the fridge magnet page does still have a devoted following. Some regular users seem to have been using the page for over a decade. One guy has been posting the message "Its Friday time for a beer a joint and a BJ" once a week since I can remember.

Kevin's Fridge Magnets

Fridge Magnet site.

Another popular page on savetz.com was "50 Years Of Band-Aid." When we bought our house from Mitch's family, they hadn't completely cleaned it out. The garage had a workbench that was full of his great-grandfather's old tools. Inside the workbench were nails, washers, and bolts, all stored in vintage Band-Aid boxes. The boxes were really cool, so I used that poor abused scanner to take pictures of them, and put them on the Web. It was another hit of the early Web. For years, people sent me pictures of their own old Band-Aid boxes, which I added to the page. Employees from Johnson and Johnson sent me more information. The nephew of Josephine Knight, the woman for whom the Band-Aid was invented, e-mailed me with pictures and stories. I was interviewed for collectors' magazines. I was considered an expert on Band-Aid tins, basically because no one had bothered to clean out our house. (The page is still online at www.savetz.com/bandaid/)

My Band-Aid page was on the Web many years before Johnson and Johnson had its official Band-Aid site, and had racked up hundreds of links from all around the Internet. A strange result of that was my little little page was Google's top result for "band-aid" for years, outranking J&J's official site.

CLASSIC COMPUTING WEB SITES

In 1996, I occasionally wrote articles for Mac Home Journal magazine. I noticed a familiar name in the masthead: a man named Jim Capparell was the publisher. Jim had also been the publisher of Antic, one of the longest-running Atari magazines. Antic was published from 1982 until 1990.

I emailed Jim and asked for permission to make Antic available on the Web. He graciously gave permission, which was the start of a new Web site, The Digital Antic Project, at www.AtariMagazines.com. I scanned two issues of Antic, performed optical character recognition (OCR) on them, converted each article to HTML, and put them online. A handful of people from the Usenet group comp.sys.atari.8bit volunteered to help put more issues online, so we proceeded to scan, OCR, and HTMLize all 88 issues of Antic. It took a while — the last issues went online in September 2000, four years after I started the project. But we were on a roll, and by then I had made other publisher contacts. So we continued to digitize other old computer magazines, including STart (Jim's successor to Antic, which focused on the Atari ST computers), Compute!, Creative Computing, and the Tandy Whiz Kids comic books. Part educational comic book and part marketing material, those colorful comics would teach kids about computers — and maybe make young readers beg Mom and Dad for a TRS-80 Color Computer and a useful acoustic modem.

With all those other magazines at the site, the name "Digital Antic Project" was becoming increasingly inaccurate. I renamed the site to Classic Computer Magazine Archive. I decided to keep the site at www.AtariMagazines .com, even though some of the magazines weren't about Atari computers at all.

One of the early volunteers for the site was a man named Henry Hahlbohm. I never met Henry — for 14 years we only communicated via e-mail. Henry was like a tireless magazine processing machine: I would send him a pile of old magazines. He would scan them, then OCR them, proofread the text, and painstakingly convert the articles to HTML. He'd work a little each day, and would usually e-mail me a finished article every couple of days. Like the tortoise in the fairy tale, Henry wasn't particularly fast, but he was relentless. When he finished digitizing the pile of magazines, he'd send it back and ask for another. Over the years, Henry digitized thousands of articles in at least 100 magazine issues. He single-handedly archived the entire runs of some shorter-lived Atari magazines.

Henry and I didn't talk much other than about the work of digitizing Atari magazines and books. He'd tell me if he was going to be on vacation, but otherwise he wasn't a chatty fellow. I didn't know anything about him other than that helping to preserve these old magazines was obviously important to him.

In early 2011, I realized that I hadn't heard from Henry in a while. I e-mailed him asking about his progress — no reply. A few weeks later I e-mailed again, asking if he was OK — again, no answer. I sent a letter to his snail-mail address. I got a letter from the trustee of his estate: "I'm sorry to inform you that your friend died." Saddened, I Googled Henry and found his obit. Henry had studied electrical engineering at M.I.T. and was a communication specialist in the Army. He had traveled the world, and worked on many government projects including the moon landing. Apparently, Henry had had an amazing life, which I didn't know until after he was dead. If he did everything with the same quiet dedication that he had with the magazine project, I'm sure he was a force to contend with.

Working on AtariMagazines.com, I have made contacts from various publications as well as individual authors from the magazines. People search for their names and find the site — they are almost universally thrilled to find that we have saved their articles and programs online. Most no longer even have copies the programs that they had written, so are excited to be able to download them and see them again for the first time in decades. One writer even claimed he was never paid for his article, but still let me put it on the site.

The one exception was a guy who wrote a single article for Antic magazine and refused to let it go online. I removed it, so AtariMagazines.com only has 1,747 of the 1,748 articles that appeared in that magazine.

That site also led to an interesting exchange with a man who claimed to be defamed by one of the articles in Creative Computing magazine. The article, which was originally published in 1984, described a live performance that combined dancing and synthesized music. The article described a technical malfunction that caused the show to end early. The person who emailed to complain, who was mentioned by name in the article, asked that I remove a paragraph from the site because it is not true, and had adversely harmed his reputation. The request concluded with veiled threats of legal recourse if I did not comply. I pointed out that the article in question was published more than 20 years earlier, and because my Web site was an archive, deleting any portion of text from that article would be a disservice. You wouldn't remove a paragraph from archives of The New York Times at a library because it offends someone 20 years later. I told him: Right or wrong, the article is part of computing history and I would not redact it.

He wouldn't drop the issue, and finally I offered a compromise: I would replace the text of his name with an graphic of his name. That way, the article would still be readable by people, but search engines wouldn't find the name, because it was an image. He agreed and let the matter drop. My solution was a hack, but I was able to stick to my principles — and it was a cheaper solution than hiring a lawyer.

Speaking of lawyers, from time to time I am contacted by attorneys working on patent defense cases. In their research for prior art (that is, to prove that an idea existed before it was patented by someone else) they'll find a concept described in one of the articles preserved at AtariMagazines .com. Sometimes they contact me because they want a copy of the physical magazine. Sometimes they just write to say thanks. I'm happy to help.

Computer-related content ages in a strange way: it goes stale quickly, then slowly starts to get better with age. One to five years out, it's just old. Beyond that, it becomes of historical interest. With the Classic Computer Magazine Archive, I'll put anything and everything online (and leave it there forever) because it will be useful to someone, someday.

I still add material to AtariMagazines.com in fits and starts, squeezing it in between other projects. It's a fun, nostalgic way for me to keep in touch with the Atari 800-, TI 99/4A-, Apple //c-loving kid inside.

* * *

When authors and publishers contact me regarding AtariMagazines.com, I always ask if they retain rights to other classic computer related material: software or books they had written, for example. Some do, and many have graciously given me permission to make that stuff available too. So I had a little problem — a growing pile of books and software and other not-magazine material, and a Web site called AtariMagazines.com. I didn't want to add books and software (and who knows what other media would come along) to the already-inaccurately named AtariMagazines .com, so I created a new site, AtariArchives.org. That's where I'd put all the not-magazine classic computing stuff.

The volunteers and I found some great stuff to save: like the disk-based newsletter of the Old Hackers Atari User Group, which ran from 1990 to 2000. And an unfinished, unpublished book about the Action! programming language. When the Cleveland Free-Net BBS was slated to shut down in 1999 (a victim of the Y2K bug), Michael Current and I carefully archived everything in the Atari Special Interest Group and saved it at AtariArchives.org.

The majority of the material on the site, though, is books — about BASIC programming, 6502 assembly language, and related topics. My favorites include David Ahl's BASIC Computer Games books; and Digital Deli, "the Comprehensive, User-Lovable Menu of Computer Lore, Culture, Lifestyles and Fancy," which was published in 1984.

The site also has the Best of Creative Computing series of books, which were compilations with the best articles from the first few years of that magazine. The first book, at www.atariarchives.org/bcc1/, had editions with two different covers. The earlier cover featured ASCII art of Mr. Spock, while the second edition had colorful line art of a robot head … thing. I asked Ahl why the cover was changed. He answered, "The original Best of Creative Computing had Mr. Spock on the cover. However, a few years later when we needed more books, Paramount was getting nasty about the use of Star Trek characters without a proper license. Initially we were under their radar screen, but we would have had to pay them mucho $$$ for the larger press run of the reprint book, so we needed another cover. The cover illustration I used had been used on an issue of the magazine but the printer had mixed up two of the color negatives (cyan and magenta) so it looked a bit strange. Needless to say, the artist was rather unhappy with the outcome as was I, so I decided to use the same illustration, this time with the correct colors, on the cover of the book."

My favorite non-book thing at that site is probably the archive of software and catalogs from the Atari Program Exchange. Atari Program Exchange (APX) was — and remains — a rare software distribution model, in which Atari would encourage end users to create software for their computers, then would sell the software through a catalog, and pay royalties to the programmers. Part of Atari from 1982 until 1984, APX offered programs that were not as commercially viable as Atari's regular boxed software, but would still be useful for niche audiences. For instance, there was a program to teach sign language fingerspelling, many programming utilities, and an application for doing calculations for building hydraulic systems. (The author of the hydraulic utility once emailed me asking for a copy of the program: he wanted to create

The two covers of The
Best of Creative Computing
Volume 1.

an updated version for modern platforms, and wanted to review the algorithms.)

Some of the APX software was incredibly specific, like Strategic Financial Ratio Analysis, Real Estate Cash Flow, and RPN Calculator Simulator. The APX catalog also included many memorable games, including GetAway!, Galahad and the Holy Grail, and Eastern Front: 1941 — which became so popular it was re-released as an official, boxed title from Atari.

Back in the day, I just liked to read and re-read the APX catalogs, which had colorful, cartoony covers, with screenshots and detailed descriptions of each program on the inside. I'd read the descriptions of every program (even the hydraulics utility) and daydream about having my own software for sale in the APX catalog.

When I started building the APX section of AtariArchives.org, I was able to contact Fred Thorlin, who had been director of APX. He let me interview him for the Web site (the interview is at www.atariarchives.org/APX/thorlininterview.php) but also was gracious enough to try contacting all of the APX programmers using their old addresses. He sent postcards to each programmer, with a short note telling them about the Atari Archives project and asking them to contact me. Since many years had passed — this was in 2000, some 17 years after the last APX catalog was published — many of the postcards were returned undeliverable. But a few found their way to the programmers, most of who graciously agreed to share their software online.

My philosophy with AtariArchives and the computer magazine archive has always been to get permission from the rightsholders. First, I enjoy the challenge of tracking down the people who wrote those old books, magazines, and programs, then hearing their stories about creating them.

More importantly, as a writer and publisher myself, I feel that is important to respect others' copyrights. This directly contradicts all the software piracy I participated in when I was younger. What can I say? I like to ask permission before I share content on my Web sites, and I pay for the software that I use now. I wish I had a story of how I came around to stop the software piracy that was so pervasive in my youth, but it was simply a matter of growing up and developing a deeper respect for software developers and publishers.

Sometimes, my way just doesn't work: rightsholders die, or just can't be found. Or, the rightsholder can be found but says no — which usually happens when the material is owned by a corporation that is still in business.

When companies are bought, sometimes it is unclear where the rights to the material ended up. For example, the Minnesota Educational Computing Consortium produced dozens of educational software programs in the 1970s and '80s. MECC was acquired by Brøderbund, which was later acquired by The Learning Company. When I asked The Learning Company for permission to distribute MECC's old titles, I was told that the files proving that the programs actually belonged to The Learning Company were long gone. The Learning Company was unable to confirm that they in fact owned those old titles, so wouldn't grant permission. Unless an attorney stumbles on a file cabinet stuffed with those documents, the rights to dozens of MECC's educational applications are lost until their copyright expires — 95 years from when they were published.

Jason Scott — the guy who filled out so many reader service cards — has archived thousands of computer magazines and books using a different philosophy: digitize it all now, save the material while it still exists, and damn the whole asking permission thing. He says, "It's better to ask for probation than permission." It's a different philosophy of archiving than I take, but I respect it: he's ensured that a metric boatload of historical tech publications are available to everyone, forever. You can find his magazine archive at www.archive.org/details/computermagazines.

In 2005, I launched a third Web site related to classic computers: FlightSimBooks.com. It has the full text of 21 classic books about flight simulation. Once again, I had received permission to publish the books on the Web, AtariArchives.org didn't seem like a sensible home, so a new site was born.

I've always thought flight sims were interesting, ever since playing Sublogic Flight Simulator on the Apple //c. That program proved to be a constant source of frustration, but I played with it for countless hours anyway. (I never did manage to land a plane with it, though.) In 1988, my friend Robert showed me his new Amiga, and its version of Flight Simulator — which was impressive because of its speed, beautiful graphics, and how easy the simulated jet was to fly compared to the Cessna in the Apple version. As an adult, I learned to fly a real Cessna (including the landings) and earned a private pilot license. I stopped flying shortly after accomplishing that goal: it was too expensive a hobby.

Several of the books at FlightSimBooks.com are meant to be used along with Sublogic Flight Simulator or Microsoft Flight Simulator, by guiding you through flight adventures. Others are geared toward other simulators, such as F-15 Strike Eagle and F-19 Stealth Fighter from Microprose.

As a side note: I was oddly crestfallen in 2003 when the city of Chicago closed down Meigs field, the real-life airport that was the default starting runway for the early versions of Flight Simulator. Though I had never been to the real airfield, I had a fondness for it, having made hundreds of takeoffs and zero successful landings in its virtual version. Apparently the closure of the airport was a real soap opera. Quoting Wikipedia: "In 2001, a compromise was reached between Chicago, the State of Illinois, and others to keep the airport open for the next twenty-five years. However, the federal legislation component of the deal did not pass the United States Senate. In a controversial move on March 31, 2003, Mayor Daley ordered private crews to destroy the runway in the middle of the night, bulldozing large X-shaped gouges into the runway surface. The required notice was not given to the Federal Aviation Administration or the owners of airplanes tied down at the field, and as a result sixteen planes were left stranded at an airport with no operating runway, and an incoming flight was diverted. The stranded aircraft were later allowed to depart from Meigs' 3,000-foot taxiway." The city had to pay a $33,000 fine and the makers of Flight Simulator had to choose a new default airfield.

CHAPTER 13
PUBLISHER

It's not too often that you can point to an event and say "that thing, that changed my life." For me, one of those events was being invited to join a mastermind group. A mastermind group is a club made up of successful people who have something in common. In this case, the group I was invited to was for self-employed Internet entrepreneurs. Between writing for online publications and my Web sites, I felt I qualified, and apparently the other members agreed, because I was accepted in February 2005.

Having online discussions with the smart, successful business owners in the group was great. But the real life-changing part was when I met the others in the group in person for the first time. We have conferences twice a year, in a different city each time. My first conference was in Atlanta, Georgia, and that's where I met Tim Carter.

Tim Carter is a gregarious guy, always smiling and always willing to share his many opinions. He runs AskTheBuilder.com, a Web site about home improvement. The first time I met him, less than one minute into our first conversation, he called me an idiot to my face — and changed my business and my life.

I'm the new guy, feeling overwhelmed in a room full of new people who all already know each other, trying to remember names and not to feel out of place.

Tim: "Hi, I'm Tim."
Me: "Nice to meet you, I'm Kevin."
Tim: "What do you do?"
Me: "I have some Web sites, but mostly I'm a freelance technology writer —"
Tim: "You're an IDIOT!"
Me: "...Uhhhhh?"

I would find out that Tim's rant was more than just abusing the new guy: he had been a syndicated newspaper columnist for many years (writing about home improvement, naturally). He is a master carpenter and has also spent decades building and remodeling homes. Tim thought I was an idiot because I was trading my time for money. I put in my time writing an article, which turned into cash. His point was that even if I was getting $1,000 an hour for writing (and I was getting nowhere near that,) because there are only so many hours in a day, the amount of money I could make was limited.

After I got over the shock of meeting Tim and everyone else, I thought about what he meant. A Web site can make money at three in the morning when I'm sleeping. Or when I'm playing in the yard with my daughter. A writer can only earn while he's writing. I was making enough as a writer. What appealed to me was removing the direct link between hours spent working and income. Earning so-called passive income was appealing: it would be nice to be able to take a few days off and know that we'd still be able to afford luxuries such as food and electricity.

My Web sites already were earning some money through advertisements, and most of them were hobby sites. I decided to invest less time in freelance writing and spend more of my time trying to make my Web sites a real business. Over the next few months, I gradually accepted fewer magazine assignments, and when regular columns dried up, I didn't bother to replace them with other writing work. I was lucky that I could make that — possibly dangerous — transition slowly rather than jumping off a cliff; it's not like I had to face a boss and say, "I quit! I'm going to publish Web sites."

That's how I made the switch from a freelance writer with some Web sites to a Web publisher. By the end of my 14-year writing career, I had written well over 1,000 articles.

Tim and I are good friends. He has apologized to me over and over for his behavior when we first met, but I appreciate what happened. He woke me up to a new possibility that I might not have fully embraced otherwise.

I figured that part out, but I still haven't figured out how to succinctly explain to people what I do. Most people don't understand how I make my living. Calling myself a Web site publisher doesn't really give people enough information. When I say "I make Web sites" the reply is inevitably "Oh, I need a new site for my business/wedding/ nonprofit" — but I don't take on clients. The answer that elicits the fewest confused looks is, "I come up with ideas for sites that provide useful information and services, and make money through advertising." The answer that I like best is "I make a living by giving stuff away."

(I'm not the only one with the problem of explaining my job. Devanie is the content director for my company, which mostly involves wrangling content for the free printables sites. Her grandma doesn't understand her job and tells her friends that Devanie is "the editor of the Internet.")

I love that my business provides real value to people. Every weekday, 6,000 to 7,000 people don't have to drive to Kinko's to send a fax, because they use my Web site, FaxZero.com, instead. Ninety-five percent of them don't even pay to do it. Every day of the year, people download 30,000 forms and other templates from the FreePrintable.net sites, saving themselves — what? — an hour of frustration creating it themselves (if they have the know-how to do it at all). The vast majority get those forms for free.

FaxZero is one of my most popular Web sites. It lets you send a fax from your computer for free, or for a couple of dollars, depending on the features that you need.

I'd had the idea for a free Internet faxing service for a long time: in my work on the fax FAQ, people often asked how they could send a fax for free. At the time, there was just one service that did it, called tpc.int. It was a volunteer-run service that had spotty coverage: you could only fax certain cities. I thought it should be possible to have a free service that let you send a fax anywhere in the United States. Because of the fax FAQ, I had contacts at every one of the companies that offered subscription-based Internet fax services. I told the owners of several companies that there was a real need for a free faxing service, and that I thought it could be profitable. They each ignored my advice. I suppose they said to themselves, "Why should we give away a service that competes with the service we're selling?"

I might not have created the site at all, except for the fact that one night in 2006, I couldn't sleep. I got out of bed, went to the computer, and started searching for domain names for new Web sites. I loved bulk domain name search tools. I still love them. It gives you a big box where you can type ideas for domain names, and it quickly tells you which are available and which aren't. I probably searched for hundreds of domains that night. In one of the bulk searches, I typed: FAX1, FAX2, FAX3, and so on, up to FAX0. It said FAX0.COM was available, and I liked the sound of it. I quickly grabbed FaxZero.com too.

Now that I had the domain names, what was I going to do with them? FaxZero seemed like the perfect name to go along with my old free faxing site idea. I did things kind of backward — buying the domain name then creating a business around it — instead of the sensible thing, having a business idea first. (I suppose this kind of behavior is why today I have more than 600 domain names.)

I hired overseas programmers through Elance.com to build the FaxZero site and backend for under $800. The job they did was good enough, but just barely. The important thing was that it worked. Then I went to GotLogos.com and had them create the FaxZero logo, which cost $25. Six years and six million transmitted faxes later, that logo still adorns the top of the site. It kind of looks like a $25 logo, but it has done its job admirably.

Since then, several other sites have duplicated the FaxZero business model, including a couple of the companies that passed on the idea when I tried to give it to them. In 2011, a new company offering a service very similar to FaxZero received thousands of dollars in seed funding from YCombinator. I kind of boggled at that. I created FaxZero for something like $825. But I was lucky, and frugal.

I built FaxZero with no market research, or business plan, or deep consideration of whether it would be profitable. I just had a gut feeling that it would be a useful Web site that people would want to use. I'm a believer in "scratching my own itch" — if I think a Web site will be useful, other people will probably think so also.

That has more or less been my M.O. for all the Web sites that I've created. Projected income statements and break even analyses and pricing strategies are deathly boring to me: I didn't do them for FaxZero, or ever. I picked a price for the paid option on FaxZero — $1.99 for up to 15 pages, only because it felt right. I'm not saying this is how you should start a business. I'm pretty sure it's a terrible way to start a business, but it has worked for me.

That is, sometimes it has worked for me. It didn't work with ReviewRoundup.com, my site that was supposed to aggregate reviews of consumer products. I spent thousands of dollars on a custom content management system and on having review abstracts written, before finding out that the site wasn't going to get the traffic that it needed to survive. It hasn't worked so well with BetterOCR.com, my service that adds human proofreading to optical character recognition. That site is still up and gets some use, though it hasn't been a big win.

One of my first itch-scratching Web sites was Free After Rebate, a blog where we posted products we found that were free after a mail-in rebate. I created the site on a whim in December 2003 because I was getting tired of looking at a dozen different sources, each of which might list one or two freebies each week, to find the deals. I decided that if I was going to be making the effort to find free-after-rebate deals, I might as well share my finds. I registered FreeAfterRebate.info and installed a blog management backend called GeekLog — this was before WordPress had gained a foothold as the de facto starter blog. It turned out that I wasn't the only one who wanted to know about free-after-rebate stuff: the site started to get traffic, so I coded a rebate calendar, so people could grab the deals that were expiring soon, and created a guide to getting the most out of rebates. The site was updated until 2008: by then, manufacturers were moving away from rebate freebies — there just weren't many deals to post anymore.

If a project seems interesting to me, and profitable, and it will be useful to people, I'll create it. Actually, any two of those three is good enough. Perhaps I'm not just a terrible nerd, but a terrible businessman as well. Either way, it's worked for me.

My other popular site is www.FreePrintable.net, which is actually an umbrella for 85 sites, all of which offer printable documents and templates. For instance, www. FreePrintableCertificates.net offers award certificates, and www.PrintableSigns.net has thousands of signs and placards. The printables project started in 2005 with one site, FreeFaxCoverSheets.net. Printable stationery and business card sites followed shortly after.

As the sites started to get traffic, people would send suggestions asking for more printable items: receipts and resumes and business plans and calendars. I hired a designer, then two, to help create them. Combined, the FreePrintable.net sites offer more than 25,000 free documents and templates. Some of the sites offer paid versions of the documents as an option, an innovation that was Peace's idea. For instance, the PDF version of a printable certificate is free, but the editable .DOC version costs $5. I'm the same lousy salesman I was at Video Concepts: if the $5 version is what the user needs, fantastic — but if they just download the free version and leave my site happy, that's great too. Every week I get a pile of e-mails from around the world from people thanking me for the help in their classrooms, churches, and small businesses. It's very gratifying.

CHAPTER 14
VINTAGE COMPUTERS

y collection of old computers has grown and shrunk and grown again over the years. At one point, I had at least 80 machines — from common models like Commodore 16 and IBM PCjr to obscure machines like the Oric-1 and Tomy Tutor. I bought them at thrift stores, yard sales, Usenet, and on eBay. There were old computers stashed all over the house: in the attic, in the closets, in the garage, and a few out on display.

Eventually the collection seemed to become too much. I felt overwhelmed by all the old computers everywhere, many of which didn't work perfectly or were missing software or some other key component to make them useful. I didn't have the time or inclination to play with all of those machines, so why did I have them? I made the decision to drastically cut down my collection, pruning it back to the machines that I had a personal connection to: primarily, the Atari 8-bit machines.

In October 2002 I rented a van, crammed it dangerously full of those old computers, and drove seven or eight hours south to the fifth annual Vintage Computer Festival conference in Mountain View, California. I attended VCF every year, but this was the first time I had gotten a vendor's table. I was going to sell those old computers to other people who would appreciate them.

My single vendor's table expanded to take up three long tables, plus the space under, above and around them. The amount of gadgetry bordered on insanity. A guy named Erik Klein was there and posted pictures of the mess on his Web site (www.vintage-computer.com/vcf5.shtml). It takes five photos to show the full spread of the stuff I had to sell.

Looking at the pictures now, I remember exactly where I acquired some of that equipment. The Adam disk drive — pretty rare, still in the box — came from a thrift store in Southern California. Mitch had given me the NeXT "pizza box" workstation. Somewhere in the pile is an HP desktop calculator that I bought at a thrift store for just a few bucks. This particular thrift store sold products by weight: you'd put your finds on an industrial scale and pay 50 cents a pound; it didn't matter if it was clothes or electronics. My six-pound, $3 calculator was worth $300 or so to an HP calculator collector.

In the pictures you can also see a piano keyboard accessory for the Intellivision. I had gotten the keyboard in a terrible online trade — ugh, I got taken.

A few years earlier, I had found a demonstration cartridge for the RCA Studio II video game system, in a dirty, basement thrift store in Eureka, California. This was an extremely rare cart, in its original box, for one of the earliest home game consoles. I didn't care much about Studio II games, but I was working hard to collect everything for the Intellivision — a system that remains close to my heart. So I traded the like-new-in-box demo cart for the Intellivision piano keyboard, a peripheral that was certainly not common, but wasn't anything like the rare gem that was the demo cart. Now I was trying to sell the music keyboard.

I regret letting some of that stuff go, but I suppose it was for the best. There's a fuzzy line between being a collector of old computers and being the focus of an episode of Hoarders. By limiting myself to — mostly — being an Atari 8-bit computer collector, there's a lot less opportunity for

Just a portion of the things I had for sale at the 2002 Vintage Computer Festival.

me to be the nutty guy on TV who has computers stacked to the ceiling.

I don't want to imply that I only have Atari machines now — that wouldn't be true. Right now in my basement there's a TRS-80 model I, three Kaypros that a lawyer back in Blue Lake gave to me, a C64 and a VIC-20, the BeBox, and some other machines. I enjoy using all of them from time to time.

The Atari computers are the heart of my collection: I've got at least one of each model (400, 800, 600XL, 800XL, 1200XL, 65XE, and 130XE) plus a few rarities. Those include an Atari 1200, which is a prototype version of the 1200XL; an 800XE, which was only released in Germany and Poland; and a 65XE with an Arabic keyboard and ROM chips. I also have an 1090 expansion system, which is a upgrade that was never released. The unit I have is the one that appeared in the Atari catalogs. But Atari never released any cards for it, so all it's just a pretty paperweight.

The Holy Grails for most Atari 8-bit collectors — can there be more than one Holy Grail? For Atari computer collectors, there are two — are the 1400XL and 1450XLD. These would have been the last generation of Atari's 8-bit machines, but they were never officially released. When Atari decided to drop the 8-bit line, it dumped whatever stock of the new generation machines that were on hand. There are stories that piles of them were unloaded in the bargain bins at Federated Electronics stores. Today, those bargain bin Ataris are extremely rare. A few weeks before I wrote this, a 1400XL and 1450XLD were put up for auction on eBay, but the seller abruptly ended the auction before they sold.

My collection of Atari stuff is nothing compared to that of my friend Curt Vendel, who runs the site AtariMuseum .com and is writing a trilogy of books about the history of Atari. As I write this, he's finishing the first of the three, funded via a Kickstarter campaign. Curt's collection of Atari computers, artifacts, and ephemera would make any old-school Atari lover drool. I asked him how he acquired all of that stuff. "It came from many different sources," he said. "First were from employees I found and contacted in late 1984–1985 when I called into Atari Corp. pretending to be a third-party hardware developer and asked to be transferred to engineering. Later stuff came from finding items on newsgroups, through posting ads, taking trips out to California and dumpster-diving behind Atari Corp. In fact, when Atari Corp. officially announced its closing was when the biggest dumpster dive occurred. It took three to four days to fully clear out and move all of the stuff from a massive overflowing dumpster when [the office at] 1196 Borregas closed. I still acquire items today from the network of former Atari employees who contact me and let me know things they've turned up."

I asked Curt why he is so interested in the Atari company and hardware. "I always loved Atari, its arcade games were great, they always seemed to be the best designed, always looked better than the competitors. To me, Atari was perfect, they could do no wrong and I was in love with everything the company made. When I found out the company changed hands, I patiently waited for the new computers and game console to come out, only to find out they were canceled or on hold, but I knew they existed. I saw magazine articles, photos, hands-on reports, so I knew this stuff existed and I wanted it and I made it a goal to find them and obtain them."

I asked him about the most interesting pieces in his collection, but Curt has a hard time choosing. One of them is the 1450XLD computer — one of the Grails that I mentioned earlier. "It works and it a great machine, but its case is not sturdy and I tend to wonder how Atari was going to address that. If you put a monitor on it, after 1–2 hours it begins to bend and the case puts pressure on the 7 key, so obviously the design was going to need some kind of cage or reinforcement."

"It stands out like a sore thumb, yet I rarely take notice of it — this 6-foot-tall Digital Equipment Corp VAX minicomputer that I found in Seattle that still had the 'Property of Atari Corporation' asset tag on it. That one certainly gets a lot of stares and attention when people come into my office."

LIVING COMPUTER MUSEUM

No one's collection of vintage computers could possibly compare to Paul Allen's. I was recently headed to Seattle for a conference. I had heard that Paul Allen — the multi-billionaire Microsoft co-founder — had a computer museum in Seattle, so of course I wanted to visit it. But the Living Computer Museum's Web site (www.

livingcomputermuseum.com) was strange — the address for the museum wasn't shown, nor were there open hours. However, you could fill out a form to request a visit, which I did. The curator set me up with a time for a tour.

When I arrived for my tour, the experience was surreal. I was the only person on the tour — being shown around by the museum's curator, the archivist, and the system maintenance guy. It was just me and three of them: I had their full attention for an hour and a half, as they showed me working PDPs and VAX machines, an Altair, a Xerox Alto, and other early minicomputers. They seemed pleased to show me the machines and describe their architecture in intimate and excruciating detail.

As I understand it, the computer museum used to be Paul Allen's private collection of computers. When you're a multi-billionaire, I guess having a private collection means buying a building, filling it with computers, then hiring a small staff to maintain them. It's still his collection, but he's apparently working to make it a more public collection, a real computer museum with open-to-the-public exhibits. But for now, in the interim, it's available for tours by appointment.

You can also request an account on any of several of Mr. Allen's computers, in case you feel the need to play DECWAR on an actual DEC PDP running Tops-10. (Which, naturally, is a need that I feel from time to time.)

The tour guides showed me everything on the massive third floor of the building. I wasn't invited to see the second floor, which apparently was filled with items waiting to be cataloged by the museum's new archivist. The first floor will be a lobby and atrium area. All I can really talk about is what I saw on the third floor, but the interesting part to me is that the computers there were the ones that he used back in the day. The computers I collect are the ones that I used back in the day. I think it's like that with most people who collect vintage computers or train sets or Barbie dolls or anything else. There's just something magical about having a little bit of your youth. Perhaps it reminds people of the good times when they were young. Or perhaps those computers, trains, or dolls were the only good things in a crappy world of crappiness. Or perhaps we find joy in being a grown-up with a job, and being able to have all the stuff we wanted but couldn't have when we were kids. Maybe it's one of those things, or something else. All I know is: I have my collection of Ataris in the basement, and Paul Allen has his collection of DECs and other industrial-refrigerator-sized computers up in Seattle. They just aren't in his basement.

CHAPTER 15
EPILOGUE

In August of 2010, my family and I moved to Portland, Oregon which is an awesome city, and not a bad place at all to be a retrogaming and retrocomputing nerd. Portland is home to Ground Kontrol, a fantastic arcade with a ton of classic games like Tron and Missile Command. (www.groundkontrol.com) Show up on the right night of the month, and you can play all night for just the $5 cover charge.

Portland is also home to Powell's Books, the largest independent bookstore anywhere: four stories and an entire city block of new and used books. Which is great, but technophiles like me walk across the street to Powells 2, which is devoted to books on computing, sciences, mathematics, and other nerdy things. You can walk in there any day of the week and find computer books from the 1980s and electronics books from the 1950s. It's nerdvana.

Portland has two Commodore groups: the PDX Commodore Users group (pdxcug.org) and the Commodore Computer Club (commodorecomputerclub.com). Technically those meetings are across the bridge in Vancouver, Washington but I'll give credit to Portland anyway.

Also here: VintageTEK (vintagetek.org), a museum devoted to vintage Tektronix equipment and memorabilia from the company's heyday, 1946–1985. Tektronix creates electronic tools and test equipment like oscilloscopes and logic analyzers, and its employees have created a ton of well-known spin-off companies.

The annual Portland Retro Gaming Expo (retrogaming-expo.com) is a dream for people like me who like games from "back in the day," offering a weekend of buying, selling, and playing of all manner of vintage video gaming goodness, plus the chance to meet alumni from companies such as Activision. My first PRGE was in 2010, just a few days after my family moved to Portland. We hadn't even unpacked most of the boxes we had moved from California. I felt a little guilty bringing another box of vintage computers and games home from that show.

At that con, I watched a guy named Bill Carlton give a talk about his attempt to break the Missile Command world record. He was up on stage, playing a Missile Command arcade game while he gave his presentation. Wave after wave of ICBMs rained down on his cities — he knocked them all out of the sky as he casually chatted with the audience. It was impressive.

But none of those things are specifically why I love Portland. We moved here because after 20 years in Arcata and Blue Lake, California, Peace and I were ready for a change of scenery. We were ready for a place that was less rural, and we wanted more opportunities for our kids. We visited Portland in the summer of 2010 to see a show (W00tstock — a night of geeks and music) and fell in love with the city. Two weeks later we came back and bought a house.

So here we are today. I run my business from my home office. On my desk there's the iMac where I make Web sites — but there's always an Atari computer on the desk too, as well as some other vintage computer, which I rotate out depending on my mood. (Currently it's an Apple //e.)

WHERE ARE THEY NOW?

Here's the current status of some of the people and computers that I've mentioned.

Mom lives in Arizona, and has been happily married to George — the guy she met in the America Online chat room — for 15 years. She just bought an iPad, so maybe she's starting to change her mind on the while Apple vs. PC thing.

Dad is retired, volunteers at a high school, and handles the tech support for FaxZero.com.

Danny, who stayed up late hacking BBS code with me, now works at Google, and still loves to stay up late hacking. We meet up every year at the California Extreme video game show.

Mitch, former system administrator of the 3B2/400 and my college roommate, is now systems administrator for a big dot.com. He has a bevy of classic arcade games in his garage, no tokens necessary.

Of the girls I've mentioned in the book: Beth, the terrible starter girlfriend, lives in Mississippi and owns a ceramics store. Kim, the red-headed skater chick, is now a red-headed vice-president of a bank. Peace, who owned a VIC-20, and I have been married for 18 years and have two wonderful daughters. She lost her BASIC level 2 programmer card somewhere along the way, but I still like her.

Dad's Atari 800 is still with me, and it still likes to play Jumpman.

My first Mac, the IIsi, was replaced by a Mac IIci, then a PowerComputing PowerTower 180 (a Mac clone,) then a Power Mac G4, then a Mac Pro, then an iMac with beautiful 27" screen.

STUFF THAT I LIKE THAT YOU MIGHT LIKE

Now that you've finished my book, here's some other nerdy books, movies, and Web sites that you might enjoy.

BOOKS AND MAGAZINES

The Happiest Days of Our Lives by Wil Wheaton. Wil was just like me — a nerdy kid growing up in Southern California in the '70s and '80s. Well, except he was Wesley on Star Trek: The Next Generation. Another great book he wrote: Just A Geek. (www.wilwheaton books.com)

Commodork: Sordid Tales from a BBS Junkie by Rob O'Hara. '80s Kid has fun with computers. It's sort of the Commodore geek kid version of this book. (www .robohara.com/commodork/)

Juiced.GS: a quarterly print magazine for Apple II users. (www.juiced.gs)

2600: The Hacker Quarterly. Hacking magazine continuously published since 1984. I've got a lifetime subscription (a fact that I'll bet, somewhere in Washington, D.C., is enshrined in a little folder).

MOVIES

Get Lamp by Jason Scott. A documentary about text adventure games. (www.getlamp.com)

BBS Documentary by Jason Scott. A documentary about bulletin board systems. (www.bbsdocumentary.com)

WarGames. The movie that almost kept me from getting online at all. I'm talking the original from 1983. Don't fall for any crappy remake.

Tron. Still one of my favorites. I'm talking the original from 1982. All right, fine. The sequel, Tron: Legacy from 2010 is pretty damn good too. (And has a fantastic soundtrack.)

EMULATORS

Atari800MacX. The open-source Atari 800 emulator for Mac that I like the best. (www.atarimac.com/atari800macx .php) For the ultra-geeky retro hobbyist, the same programmer created SIO2OSX, a peripheral emulator that allows a real Atari computer to use a Mac as as its disk drive, cassette drive, and printer. (www.atarimac .com/sio2osx.php)

Virtual Apple. (www.virtualapple.org) A complete Apple // emulator in your browser. Amazing.

Multi Emulator Super System. MESS lets your computer emulate 570+ different systems, including Intellivision, Channel F, Commodore 64, TRS-80, and so many more. It works on Mac, Windows, and Linux. (www.mess.org)

Frotz (frotz.sourceforge.net) Play classic and modern interactive fiction on your iPhone or iPad. Search for it in the App Store.

WEB SITES

www.AtariAge.com. The go-to community for Atari computer users.

Society for the Promotion of Adventure Games. SPAG is a quarterly e-zine covering interactive fiction. (www .sparkynet.com/spag/)

Classic Computer Magazine Archive (www.AtariMagazines .com) My site, with 20,000+ articles from old computer magazines.

AtariArchives.org. Another of my sites, with the full text of many classic computer books.